Apache Spark Quick Start Guide

Quickly learn the art of writing efficient big data applications
with Apache Spark

Shrey Mehrotra
Akash Grade

BIRMINGHAM - MUMBAI

Apache Spark Quick Start Guide

Commissioning Editor: Amey Varangaonkar
Acquisition Editor: Siddharth Mandal
Content Development Editor: Smit Carvalho
Technical Editor: Aishwarya More
Copy Editor: Safis Editing
Project Coordinator: Pragati Shukla
Proofreader: Safis Editing
Indexer: Pratik Shirodkar
Graphics: Alishon Mendonsa
Production Coordinator: Deepika Naik

First published: January 2019

Production reference: 1310119

Published by Packt Publishing Ltd.
Livery Place
35 Livery Street
Birmingham
B3 2PB, UK.

ISBN 978-1-78934-910-8

www.packtpub.com

`mapt.io`

Mapt is an online digital library that gives you full access to over 5,000 books and videos, as well as industry leading tools to help you plan your personal development and advance your career. For more information, please visit our website.

Why subscribe?

- Spend less time learning and more time coding with practical eBooks and videos from over 4,000 industry professionals

- Improve your learning with Skill Plans built especially for you

- Get a free eBook or video every month

- Mapt is fully searchable

- Copy and paste, print, and bookmark content

Packt.com

Did you know that Packt offers eBook versions of every book published, with PDF and ePub files available? You can upgrade to the eBook version at `www.packt.com` and as a print book customer, you are entitled to a discount on the eBook copy. Get in touch with us at `customercare@packtpub.com` for more details.

At `www.packt.com`, you can also read a collection of free technical articles, sign up for a range of free newsletters, and receive exclusive discounts and offers on Packt books and eBooks.

Contributors

About the authors

Shrey Mehrotra has over 8 years of IT experience and, for the past 6 years, has been designing the architecture of cloud and big-data solutions for the finance, media, and governance sectors. Having worked on research and development with big-data labs and been part of Risk Technologies, he has gained insights into Hadoop, with a focus on Spark, HBase, and Hive. His technical strengths also include Elasticsearch, Kafka, Java, YARN, Sqoop, and Flume. He likes spending time performing research and development on different big-data technologies. He is the coauthor of the books *Learning YARN* and *Hive Cookbook*, a certified Hadoop developer, and he has also written various technical papers.

Akash Grade is a data engineer living in New Delhi, India. Akash graduated with a BSc in computer science from the University of Delhi in 2011, and later earned an MSc in software engineering from BITS Pilani. He spends most of his time designing highly scalable data pipeline using big-data solutions such as Apache Spark, Hive, and Kafka. Akash is also a Databricks-certified Spark developer. He has been working on Apache Spark for the last five years, and enjoys writing applications in Python, Go, and SQL.

About the reviewer

Nisith Kumar Nanda is a passionate big data consultant who loves to find solutions to complex data problems. He has around 10 years of IT experience working on multiple technologies with various clients globally. His core expertise involves working with open source big data technologies such as Apache Spark, Kafka, Cassandra, HBase, to build critical next generation real-time and batch applications. He is very proficient in various programming languages such as Java, Scala, and Python. He is passionate about AI, machine learning, and NLP.

> *I would like to thank my family and especially my wife, Samita, for their support. I will also take this opportunity to thank my friends and colleagues who helped me to grow professionally.*

Packt is searching for authors like you

If you're interested in becoming an author for Packt, please visit `authors.packtpub.com` and apply today. We have worked with thousands of developers and tech professionals, just like you, to help them share their insight with the global tech community. You can make a general application, apply for a specific hot topic that we are recruiting an author for, or submit your own idea.

Table of Contents

Preface

Apache Spark is a flexible in-memory framework that allows the processing of both batch and real-time data in a distributed way. Its unified engine has made it quite popular for big data use cases.

This book will help you to quickly get started with Apache Spark 2.x and help you write efficient big data applications for a variety of use cases. You will get to grip with the low-level details as well as core concepts of Apache Spark, and the way they can be used to solve big data problems. You will be introduced to RDD and DataFrame APIs, and their corresponding transformations and actions.

This book will help you learn Spark's components for machine learning, stream processing, and graph analysis. At the end of the book, you'll learn different optimization techniques for writing efficient Spark code.

Who this book is for

If you are a big data enthusiast and love processing huge amounts of data, this book is for you. If you are a data engineer and looking for the best optimization techniques for your Spark applications, then you will find this book helpful. This book will also help data scientists who want to implement their machine learning algorithms in Spark. You need to have a basic understanding of programming languages such as Scala, Python, or Java.

What this book covers

Chapter 1, *Introduction to Apache Spark*, provides an introduction to Spark 2.0. It provides a brief description of different Spark components, including Spark Core, Spark SQL, Spark Streaming, machine learning, and graph processing. It also discusses the advantages of Spark compared to other similar frameworks.

Chapter 2, *Apache Spark Installation*, provides a step-by-step guide to installing Spark on an AWS EC2 instance from scratch. It also helps you install all the prerequisites, such as Python, Java, and Scala.

Chapter 3, *Spark RDD*, explains **Resilient Distributed Datasets** (RDD) APIs, which are the heart of Apache Spark. It also discusses various transformations and actions that can be applied on an RDD.

Chapter 4, *Spark DataFrame and Dataset,* covers Spark's structured APIs: DataFrame and Dataset. This chapter also covers various operations that can be performed on a DataFrame or Dataset.

Chapter 5, *Spark Architecture and Application Execution Flow,* explains the interaction between different services involved in Spark application execution. It explains the role of worker nodes, executors, and drivers in application execution in both client and cluster mode. It also explains how Spark creates a **Directed Acyclic Graph** (**DAG**) that consists of stages and tasks.

Chapter 6, *Spark SQL,* discusses how Spark gracefully supports all SQL operations by providing a Spark-SQL interface and various DataFrame APIs. It also covers the seamless integration of Spark with the Hive metastore.

Chapter 7, *Spark Streaming, Machine Learning, and Graph Analysis,* explores different Spark APIs for working with real-time data streams, machine learning, and graphs. It explains the candidature of features based on the use case requirements.

Chapter 8, *Spark Optimizations,* covers different optimization techniques to improve the performance of your Spark applications. It explains how you can use resources such as executors and memory in order to better parallelize your tasks.

To get the most out of this book

Use a machine with a recent version of Linux or macOS. It will be useful to know the basic syntax of Scala, Python, and Java. Install Python's NumPy package in order to work with Spark's machine learning packages.

Download the example code files

You can download the example code files for this book from your account at www.packt.com. If you purchased this book elsewhere, you can visit www.packt.com/support and register to have the files emailed directly to you.

You can download the code files by following these steps:

1. Log in or register at www.packt.com
2. Select the **SUPPORT** tab
3. Click on **Code Downloads and Errata**
4. Enter the name of the book in the **Search** box and follow the onscreen instructions

Once the file is downloaded, please make sure that you unzip or extract the folder using the latest version of:

- WinRAR/7-Zip for Windows
- Zipeg/iZip/UnRarX for Mac
- 7-Zip/PeaZip for Linux

The code bundle for the book is also hosted on GitHub at `https://github.com/PacktPublishing/Apache-Spark-Quick-Start-Guide`. In case there's an update to the code, it will be updated on the existing GitHub repository.

We also have other code bundles from our rich catalog of books and videos available at `https://github.com/PacktPublishing/`. Check them out!

Download the color images

We also provide a PDF file that has color images of the screenshots/diagrams used in this book. You can download it here: `https://www.packtpub.com/sites/default/files/downloads/9781789349108_ColorImages.pdf`.

Conventions used

There are a number of text conventions used throughout this book.

`CodeInText`: Indicates code words in text, database table names, folder names, filenames, file extensions, pathnames, dummy URLs, user input, and Twitter handles. Here is an example: "Mount the downloaded `WebStorm-10*.dmg` disk image file as another disk in your system."

Any command-line input or output is written as follows:

```
$ mkdir css
$ cd css
```

Bold: Indicates a new term, an important word, or words that you see onscreen. For example, words in menus or dialog boxes appear in the text like this. Here is an example: "Select **System info** from the **Administration** panel."

Warnings or important notes appear like this.

Tips and tricks appear like this.

Get in touch

Feedback from our readers is always welcome:

General feedback: If you have questions about any aspect of this book, mention the book title in the subject of your message and email us at customercare@packtpub.com.

Errata: Although we have taken every care to ensure the accuracy of our content, mistakes do happen. If you have found a mistake in this book, we would be grateful if you would report this to us. Please visit www.packt.com/submit-errata, selecting your book, clicking on the Errata Submission Form link, and entering the details.

Piracy: If you come across any illegal copies of our works in any form on the Internet, we would be grateful if you would provide us with the location address or website name. Please contact us at copyright@packt.com with a link to the material.

If you are interested in becoming an author: If there is a topic that you have expertise in and you are interested in either writing or contributing to a book, please visit authors.packtpub.com.

Reviews

Please leave a review. Once you have read and used this book, why not leave a review on the site that you purchased it from? Potential readers can then see and use your unbiased opinion to make purchase decisions, we at Packt can understand what you think about our products, and our authors can see your feedback on their book. Thank you!

For more information about Packt, please visit packt.com.

Introduction to Apache Spark 1

Apache Spark is an open source framework for processing large datasets stored in heterogeneous data stores in an efficient and fast way. Sophisticated analytical algorithms can be easily executed on these large datasets. Spark can execute a distributed program 100 times faster than MapReduce. As Spark is one of the fast-growing projects in the open source community, it provides a large number of libraries to its users.

We shall cover the following topics in this chapter:

- A brief introduction to Spark
- Spark architecture and the different languages that can be used for coding Spark applications
- Spark components and how these components can be used together to solve a variety of use cases
- A comparison between Spark and Hadoop

What is Spark?

Apache Spark is a distributed computing framework which makes big-data processing quite easy, fast, and scalable. You must be wondering what makes Spark so popular in the industry, and how is it really different than the existing tools available for big-data processing? The reason is that it provides a unified stack for processing all different kinds of big data, be it batch, streaming, machine learning, or graph data.

Spark was developed at UC Berkeley's AMPLab in 2009 and later came under the Apache Umbrella in 2010. The framework is mainly written in Scala and Java.

Spark provides an interface with many different distributed and non-distributed data stores, such as **Hadoop Distributed File System (HDFS)**, Cassandra, Openstack Swift, Amazon S3, and Kudu. It also provides a wide variety of language APIs to perform analytics on the data stored in these data stores. These APIs include Scala, Java, Python, and R.

The basic entity of Spark is **Resilient Distributed Dataset (RDD)**, which is a read-only partitioned collection of data. RDD can be created using data stored on different data stores or using existing RDD. We shall discuss this in more detail in Chapter 3, *Spark RDD*.

Spark needs a resource manager to distribute and execute its tasks. By default, Spark comes up with its own standalone scheduler, but it integrates easily with Apache Mesos and **Yet Another Resource Negotiator (YARN)** for cluster resource management and task execution.

One of the main features of Spark is to keep a large amount of data in memory for faster execution. It also has a component that generates a **Directed Acyclic Graph (DAG)** of operations based on the user program. We shall discuss these in more details in coming chapters.

The following diagram shows some of the popular data stores Spark can connect to:

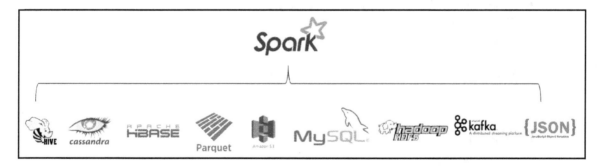

Data stores

Spark is a computing engine, and should not be considered as a storage system as well. Spark is also not designed for cluster management. For this purpose, frameworks such as Mesos and YARN are used.

Spark architecture overview

Spark follows a master-slave architecture, as it allows it to scale on demand. Spark's architecture has two main components:

- **Driver Program**: A driver program is where a user writes Spark code using either Scala, Java, Python, or R APIs. It is responsible for launching various parallel operations of the cluster.
- **Executor:** Executor is the **Java Virtual Machine** (**JVM**) that runs on a worker node of the cluster. Executor provides hardware resources for running the tasks launched by the driver program.

As soon as a Spark job is submitted, the driver program launches various operation on each executor. Driver and executors together make an *application*.

The following diagram demonstrates the relationships between **Driver**, **Workers**, and **Executors**. As the first step, a **driver** process parses the user code (**Spark Program**) and creates multiple executors on each worker node. The driver process not only forks the executors on work machines, but also sends tasks to these executors to run the entire application in parallel.

Once the computation is completed, the output is either sent to the driver program or saved on to the file system:

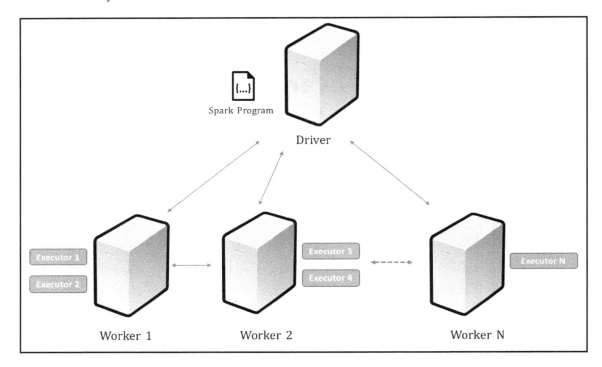

Driver, Workers, and Executors

Spark language APIs

Spark has integration with a variety of programming languages such as Scala, Java, Python, and R. Developers can write their Spark program in either of these languages. This freedom of language is also one of the reasons why Spark is popular among developers. If you compare this to Hadoop MapReduce, in MapReduce, the developers had only one choice: Java, which made it difficult for developers from another programming languages to work on MapReduce.

Scala

Scala is the primary language for Spark. More than 70% of Spark's code is written in **Scalable Language** (**Scala**). Scala is a fairly new language. It was developed by Martin Odersky in 2001, and it was first launched publicly in 2004. Like Java, Scala also generates a bytecode that runs on JVM. Scala brings advantages from both object-oriented and functional-oriented worlds. It provides dynamic programming without compromising on type safety. As Spark is primarily written in Scala, you can find almost all of the new libraries in Scala API.

Java

Most of us are familiar with Java. Java is a powerful object-oriented programming language. The majority of big data frameworks are written in Java, which provides rich libraries to connect and process data with these frameworks.

Python

Python is a functional programming language. It was developed by Guido van Rossum and was first released in 1991. For some time, Python was not popular among developers, but later, around 2006-07, it introduced some libraries such as **Numerical Python** (**NumPy**) and **Pandas**, which became cornerstones and made Python popular among all types of programmers. In Spark, when the driver launches executors on worker nodes, it also starts a Python interpreter for each executor. In the case of RDD, the data is first shipped into the JVMs, and is then transferred to Python, which makes the job slow when working with RDDs.

R

R is a statistical programming language. It provides a rich library for analyzing and manipulating the data, which is why it is very popular among data analysts, statisticians, and data scientists. Spark R integration is a way to provide data scientists the flexibility required to work on big data. Like Python, SparkR also creates an R process for each executor to work on data transferred from the JVM.

SQL

Structured Query Language (SQL) is one of the most popular and powerful languages for working with tables stored in the database. SQL also enables non-programmers to work with big data. Spark provides Spark SQL, which is a distributed SQL query engine. We will learn about it in more detail in `Chapter 6`, *Spark SQL*.

Spark components

As discussed earlier in this chapter, the main philosophy behind Spark is to provide a unified engine for creating different types of big data applications. Spark provides a variety of libraries to work with batch analytics, streaming, machine learning, and graph analysis.

It is not as if these kinds of processing were never done before Spark, but for every new big data problem, there was a new tool in the market; for example, for batch analysis, we had MapReduce, Hive, and Pig. For **Streaming**, we had Apache Storm, for machine learning, we had Mahout. Although these tools solve the problems that they are designed for, each of them requires a learning curve. This is where Spark brings advantages. Spark provides a unified stack for solving all of these problems. It has components that are designed for processing all kinds of big data. It also provides many libraries to read or write different kinds of data such as JSON, CSV, and Parquet.

Here is an example of a Spark stack:

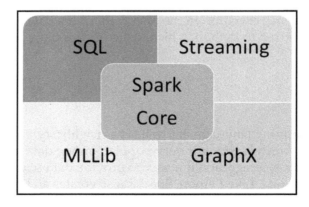

Spark stack

Having a unified stack brings lots of advantages. Let's look at some of the advantages:

- First is code sharing and reusability. Components developed by the data engineering team can easily be integrated by the data science team to avoid code redundancy.
- Secondly, there is always a new tool coming in the market to solve a different big data usecase. Most of the developers struggle to learn new tools and gain expertise in order to use them efficiently. With Spark, developers just have to learn the basic concepts which allows developers to work on different big data use cases.
- Thirdly, its unified stack gives great power to the developers to explore new ideas without installing new tools.

The following diagram provides a high-level overview of different big-data applications powered by Spark:

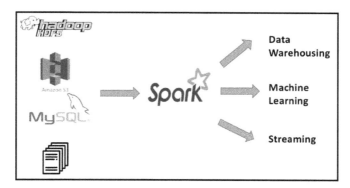

Spark use cases

Spark Core

Spark Core is the main component of Spark. Spark Core defines the following:

- The basic components, such as RDD and DataFrames
- The APIs available to perform operations on these basic abstractions
- Shared or distributed variables, such as broadcast variables and accumulators

We shall look at them in more detail in the upcoming chapters.

Spark Core also defines all the basic functionalities, such as task management, memory management, basic I/O functionalities, and more. It's a good idea to have a look at the Spark code on GitHub (`https://github.com/apache/spark`).

Spark SQL

Spark SQL is where developers can work with structured and semi-structured data such as Hive tables, MySQL tables, Parquet files, AVRO files, JSON files, CSV files, and more. Another alternative to process structured data is using Hive. Hive processes structured data stored on HDFS using **Hive Query Language** (**HQL**). It internally uses MapReduce for its processing, and we shall see how Spark can deliver better performance than MapReduce. In the initial version of Spark, structured data used to be defined as schema RDD (another type of an RDD). When there is data along with the schema, SQL becomes the first choice of processing that data. Spark SQL is Spark's component that enables developers to process data with **Structured Query Language** (**SQL**).

Using Spark SQL, business logic can be easily written in SQL and HQL. This enables data warehouse engineers with a good knowledge of SQL to make use of Spark for their **extract, transform, load** (**ETL**) processing. Hive projects can easily be migrated on Spark using Spark SQL, without changing the Hive scripts.

Spark SQL is also the first choice for data analysis and data warehousing. Spark SQL enables the data analysts to write ad hoc queries for their exploratory analysis. Spark provides Spark SQL shell, where you can run the SQL-like queries and they get executed on Spark. Spark internally converts the code into a chain of RDD computations, while Hive converts the HQL job into a series of MapReduce jobs. Using Spark SQL, developers can also make use of caching (a Spark feature that enables data to be kept in memory), which can significantly increase the performance of their queries.

Spark Streaming

Spark Streaming is a package that is used to process a stream of data in real time. There can be many different types of a real-time stream of data; for example, an e-commerce website recording page visits in real time, credit card transactions, a taxi provider app sending information about trips and location information of drivers and passengers, and more. In a nutshell, all of these applications are hosted on multiple web servers that generate event logs in real time.

Spark Streaming makes use of RDD and defines some more APIs to process the data stream in real time. As Spark Streaming makes use of RDD and its APIs, it is easy for developers to learn and execute the use cases without learning a whole new technology stack.

Spark 2.x introduced **structured streaming**, which makes use of DataFrames rather than RDD to process the data stream. Using DataFrames as its computation abstraction brings all the benefits of the DataFrame API to stream processing. We shall discuss the benefits of DataFrames over RDD in coming chapters.

Spark Streaming has excellent integration with some of the most popular data messaging queues, such as Apache Flume and Kafka. It can be easily plugged into these queues to handle a massive amount of data streams.

Spark machine learning

It is difficult to run a machine-learning algorithm when your data is distributed across multiple machines. There might be a case when the calculation depends on another point that is stored or processed on a different executor. Data can be shuffling across executors or workers, but shuffle comes with a heavy cost. Spark provides a way to avoid shuffling data. Yes, it is caching. Spark's ability to keep a large amount of data in memory makes it easy to write machine-learning algorithms.

Spark **MLlib** and **ML** are the Spark's packages to work with machine-learning algorithms. They provide the following:

- Inbuilt machine-learning algorithms such as Classification, Regression, Clustering, and more
- Features such as pipelining, vector creation, and more

The previous algorithms and features are optimized for data shuffle and to scale across the cluster.

Spark graph processing

Spark also has a component to process graph data. A graph consists of vertices and edges. Edges define the relationship between vertices. Some examples of graph data are customers's product ratings, social networks, Wikipedia pages and their links, airport flights, and more.

Spark provides **GraphX** to process such data. GraphX makes use of RDD for its computation and allows users to create vertices and edges with some properties. Using GraphX, you can define and manipulate a graph or get some insights from the graph.

GraphFrames is an external package that makes use of DataFrames instead of RDD, and defines vertex-edge relation using a DataFrame.

Cluster manager

Spark provides a *local* mode for the job execution, where both driver and executors run within a single JVM on the client machine. This enables developers to quickly get started with Spark without creating a cluster. We will mostly use this mode of job execution throughout this book for our code examples, and explain the possible challenges with a cluster mode whenever possible. Spark also works with a variety of schedules. Let's have a quick overview of them here.

Standalone scheduler

Spark comes with its own scheduler, called a **standalone scheduler**. If you are running your Spark programs on a cluster that does not have a Hadoop installation, then there is a chance that you are using Spark's default standalone scheduler.

YARN

YARN is the default scheduler of Hadoop. It is optimized for batch jobs such as MapReduce, Hive, and Pig. Most of the organizations already have Hadoop installed on their clusters; therefore, Spark provides the ability to configure it with YARN for the job scheduling.

Mesos

Spark also integrates well with Apache Mesos which is build using the same principles as the Linux kernel. Unlike YARN, Apache Mesos is general purpose cluster manager that does not bind to the Hadoop ecosystem. Another difference between YARN and Mesos is that YARN is optimized for the long-running batch workloads, whereas Mesos, ability to provide a fine-grained and dynamic allocation of resources makes it more optimized for streaming jobs.

Kubernetes

Kubernetes is as a general-purpose orchestration framework for running containerized applications. Kubernetes provides multiple features such as multi-tenancy (running different versions of Spark on a physical cluster) and sharing of the namespace. At the time of writing this book, the Kubernetes scheduler is still in the experimental stage. For more details on running a Spark application on Kubernetes, please refer to Spark's documentation.

Making the most of Hadoop and Spark

People generally get confused between Hadoop and Spark and how they are related. The intention of this section is to discuss the differences between Hadoop and Spark, and also how they can be used together.

Hadoop is mainly a combination of the following components:

- Hive and Pig
- MapReduce
- YARN
- HDFS

HDFS is the storage layer where underlying data can be stored. HDFS provides features such as the replication of the data, fault tolerance, high availability, and more. Hadoop is schema-on-read; for instance, you don't have to specify the schema while writing the data to Hadoop, rather, you can use different schemas while reading the data. HDFS also provides different types of files formats, such as `TextInputFormat`, `SequenceFile`, `NLInputFormat`, and more. If you want to know more about these file formats, I would recommend reading *Hadoop: The Definitive Guide* by Tom White.

Hadoop's MapReduce is a programming model used to process the data available on HDFS. It consists of four main phases: Map, Sort, Shuffle, and Reduce. One of the main differences between Hadoop and Spark is that Hadoop's MapReduce model is tightly coupled with the file formats of the data. On the other hand, Spark provides an abstraction to process the data using RDD. RDD is like a general-purpose container of distributed data. That's why Spark can integrate with a variety of data stores.

Another main difference between Hadoop and Spark is that Spark makes good use of memory. It can cache data in memory to avoid disk I/O. On the other hand, Hadoop's MapReduce jobs generally involve multiple disks I/O. Typically, a Hadoop job consists of multiple Map and Reduce jobs. This is known as MapReduce chaining. A MapReduce chain may look something like this: Map -> Reduce -> Map -> Map -> Reduce.

All of the reduce jobs write their output to HDFS for reliability; therefore, each map task next to it will have to read it from HDFS. This involves multiple disk I/O operations and makes overall processing slower. There have been several initiatives such as **Tez** within Hadoop to optimize MapReduce processing. As discussed earlier, Spark creates a DAG of operations and automatically optimizes the disk reads.

Apart from the previous differences, Spark complements Hadoop by providing another way of processing the data. As discussed earlier in this chapter, it integrates well with Hadoop components such as Hive, YARN, and HDFS. The following diagram shows a typical **Spark** and Hadoop ecosystem looks like. Spark makes use of **YARN** for scheduling and running its task throughout the cluster:

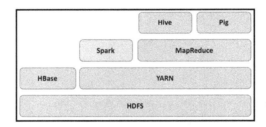

Spark and Hadoop

Summary

In this chapter, we introduced Apache Spark and its architecture. We discussed the concept of driver program and executors, which are the core components of Spark.

We then briefly discussed the different programming APIs for Spark, and its major components including Spark Core, Spark SQL, Spark Streaming, and Spark GraphX.

Finally, we discussed some major differences between Spark and Hadoop and how they complement each other. In the next chapter, we will install Spark on an AWS EC2 instance and go through different clients to interact with Spark.

Apache Spark Installation 2

In Chapter 1, *Introduction to Apache Spark*, we learned about what Spark is, its architecture, and the different components that are provided by Spark. In this chapter, we will configure Spark in different modes and look into the different APIs that we can use to access Spark clusters or to submit a Spark application. This chapter will cover the following topics:

- Creating a single node (EC2 Linux instance) on AWS cloud
- Installing Java on an instance
- Installing Python on an instance
- Installing Scala on an instance
- Installing Spark on an instance
- How to access different Spark component clients on an instance

AWS elastic compute cloud (EC2)

Amazon Web Service (**AWS**) is a popular cloud platform that provides various offerings for **infrastructure as a service** (**IAAS**), **platform as a service** (**PAAS**), and **software as a service** (**SAAS**). AWS provides scalable EC2 instances as nodes (machines) with configurable resources (RAM and cores). It also provides **Simple Storage Service** (**S3**) as scalable, low-cost storage.

Creating a free account on AWS

AWS provides you with a free account so that you can explore different services. For more details about these free services, please visit `https://aws.amazon.com/free`. You will see the following screen:

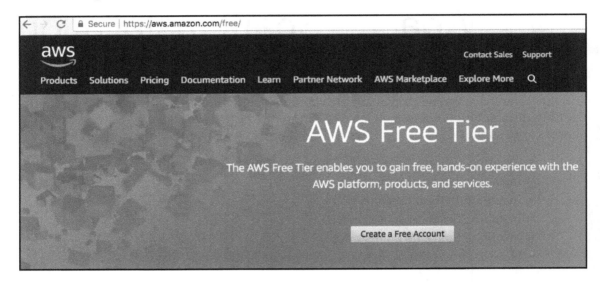

Follow these steps to get your free EC2 node for Spark installation:

1. Sign up for an AWS account with your **Email address** and **Password,** as shown in the following screenshot:

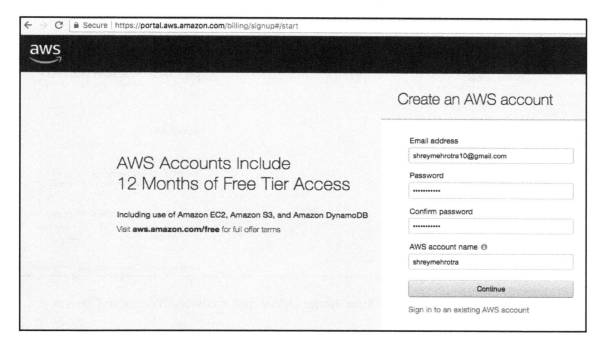

2. You will end up in the **AWS Management Console,** as follows:

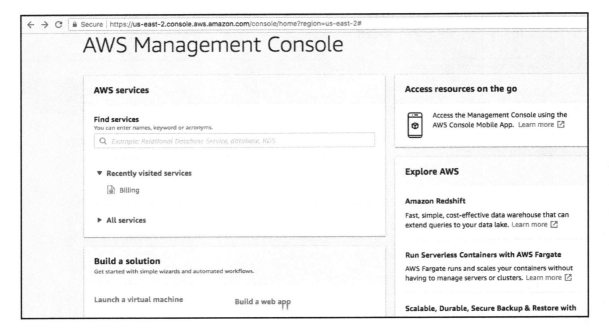

3. Select the **Amazon Machine Image (AMI)** that you want. We chose **Ubuntu Server 18.04** here:

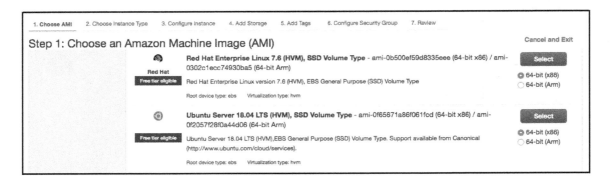

4. Select **Free tier eligible**, **t2.micro**, as follows:

5. Select **Configure Security Group** to allow all machines to connect to the instance that you've created, as follows:

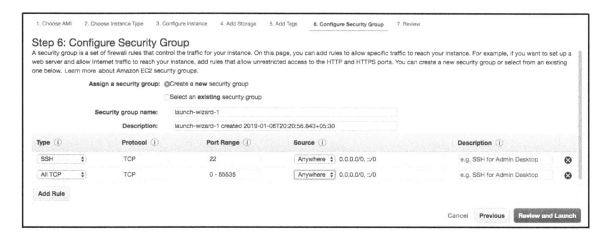

6. Review your launch instance, as follows:

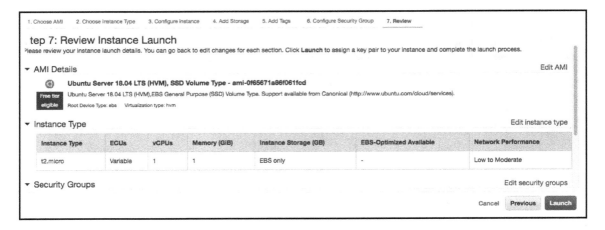

7. On clicking **Launch**, you will see a pop-up, which will allow you to generate a new key-value pair for your instance:

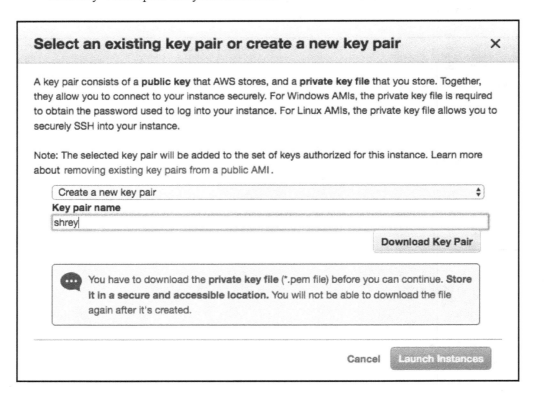

8. This will generate a public key and private keys for your instance. The public key is stored in an Amazon instance, while you need to download the private key.

9. Click on **Download Key Pair**. This will download a .pem file on to your machine. Keep it in a safe location on your machine.

10. After downloading the .pem file, click on **Launch**. This will take some time and show up the following page:

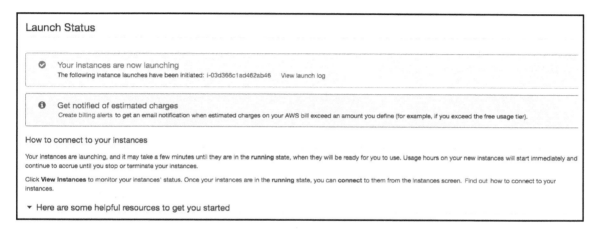

11. You can go through some helpful resources at the bottom of this page. Once your instance has started, you can check the EC2 dashboard:

Connecting to your Linux instance

Refer to the following links to connect to your instance from different platforms:

Platform	Reference
Linux	Connecting to Your Linux Instance Using SSH
Windows	Connecting to Your Linux Instance from Windows Using PuTTY Connecting to Your Linux Instance from Windows Using Windows Subsystem for Linux
All	Connecting to Your Linux Instance Using MindTerm

Once you download the `.pem` file, apply the following permission settings to get information about your machine:

- Set the permission of the `.pem` file to `400` and provide a complete path in the `ssh` command
- The default username for Ubuntu AMI is `ubuntu`
- **ec2-18-219-82-165.us-east-2.compute.amazonaws.com** is the host name of the instance

  You can get the hostname (**Public DNS (IPv4)**) and other machine details from the EC2 instance dashboard:

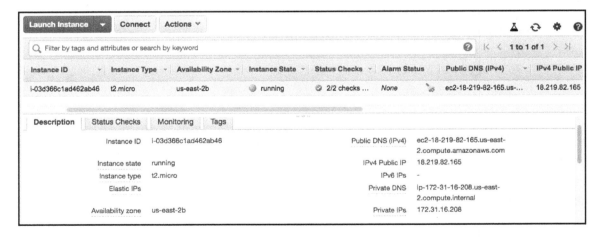

For the instance we have created, we can connect to the machine with the following commands:

```
chmod 400 shrey.pem

ssh -i "shrey.pem" ubuntu@ec2-18-219-82-165.us-east-2.compute.amazonaws.com
```

You will see the following screen upon executing the previous commands:

```
shrey:Downloads shrey$ ssh -i "shrey.pem" ubuntu@ec2-18-219-82-165.us-east-2.compute.amazonaws.com
Welcome to Ubuntu 18.04.1 LTS (GNU/Linux 4.15.0-1021-aws x86_64)

 * Documentation:  https://help.ubuntu.com
 * Management:     https://landscape.canonical.com
 * Support:        https://ubuntu.com/advantage

  System information as of Sun Jan  6 17:41:26 UTC 2019

  System load:  0.0                Processes:              87
  Usage of /:   13.4% of 7.69GB    Users logged in:        1
  Memory usage: 14%                IP address for eth0: 172.31.16.208
  Swap usage:   0%

 * MicroK8s is Kubernetes in a snap. Made by devs for devs.
   One quick install on a workstation, VM, or appliance.

   - https://bit.ly/microk8s

 * Full K8s GPU support is now available!

   - https://blog.ubuntu.com/2018/12/10/using-gpgpus-with-kubernetes


  Get cloud support with Ubuntu Advantage Cloud Guest:
    http://www.ubuntu.com/business/services/cloud

0 packages can be updated.
0 updates are security updates.


Last login: Sun Jan  6 15:46:16 2019 from 223.225.84.26
To run a command as administrator (user "root"), use "sudo <command>".
See "man sudo_root" for details.

ubuntu@ip-172-31-16-208:~$
```

Once you login to your Amazon instance, your machine will be ready to install the required frameworks.

Configuring Spark

Apache Spark can be configured in the following modes:

- Standalone mode
- Distributed or cluster mode

Prerequisites

The following are the prerequisites that are required for configuring Spark in any of the modes:

- **Linux OS**: Spark is most compatible with any flavor of the Linux operating system. You can use any desktop, virtual machine, server, or a cloud-scale machine to install Spark. Although you can install it on your Windows machine, we are using the Ubuntu AWS machine for configuring Spark.

- **Scala/Python/Java**: Spark supports APIs in multiple languages including Scala, Python, and Java. All Spark actions and transformations APIs are available in these different languages.

Installing Java

You can use the following commands to install Java on your system:

```
sudo add-apt-repository ppa:webupd8team/java -y

sudo apt install java-common oracle-java8-installer oracle-java8-set-
default
```

Installing Scala

If you have the Scala `.tar` file (for example, `scala-2.12.6.tgz`), then copy it to an AWS EC2 Linux instance at any location (for example, `/opt`):

- You can also download the latest binary `.tar.gz` file from `http://www.scala-lang.org/download/all.html`
- You can download 2.12.6 from the following location: `https://downloads.lightbend.com/scala/2.12.6/scala-2.12.6.tgz`

The `/opt` file is an empty folder within the root in most Linux-based operating folders. Here, we can use this folder to copy and install software. By default, this folder is owned by root. Run the following command if you are getting permission issues while accessing this folder:

```
sudo chmod -R 777 /opt
```

Follow these steps to install Scala 2.12.6 on your Linux VM:

1. Go to the location where you copied the Scala software package and uncompress it:

```
cd /opt
tar -xzvf scala-2.12.6.tgz
```

2. Set the environment variable in `.bash_profile`, as follows:

```
nano ~/.bash_profile
```

3. Add the following lines to the end of the file:

```
export SCALA_HOME=/opt/scala-2.12.6
export PATH=$PATH:$SCALA_HOME/bin
```

4. Run the following command to update the environment variables in the current session:

```
source ~/.bash_profile
```

5. Check for a Scala installation by running the following command:

```
scala -version
```

Installing Python

Python on Linux can be easily installed with the following commands:

```
sudo apt-get update
sudo apt-get install python3.6
```

Installing Spark

Follow these steps to install Spark 2.3.1, compiled with Hadoop 2.7:

1. If you have a Spark 2.0 tar distribution (for example, `spark-2.3.1-bin-hadoop2.7.tgz`), then copy it into your Linux VM at any location (for example, `/opt`) using any Windows on Linux file transfer software (FileZilla or WinSCP). Alternatively, you can download the latest binary `.tar.gz` file from the following Apache Spark link: `http://spark.apache.org/downloads.html`.

The /opt file is an empty folder within root in most Linux-based operating folders. Here, we would use this folder to copy and install software. By default, this folder is owned by Root. So, run the following command if you are getting permission issues while accessing this folder. sudo chmod -R 777 /opt.

2. Go to the location where you have copied the Spark software package and uncompress it:

```
cd /opt
tar -xzvf spark-2.3.1-bin-hadoop2.7.tgz
```

3. Set the environment variable in .bash_profile, as follows:

```
nano ~/.bash_profile
```

4. Add the following lines to the end of the file:

```
export SPARK_HOME=/opt/spark-2.3.1-bin-hadoop2.7
export PATH=$PATH:$SPARK_HOME/sbin
export PATH=$PATH:$SPARK_HOME/bin
```

5. Run the following command to update the environment variables in the current session:

```
source ~/.bash_profile
```

Using Spark components

Spark provides a different command-line interface, that is **read–eval–print loop** (**REPL**) for different programming languages. You can choose the type of REPL from the following, based on the language of your choice:

1. **Spark shell for Scala**: If you want to use Scala for accessing Spark APIs, you can start the Spark Scala shell with the following command:

```
spark-shell
```

The following screen will be displayed after the execution of the previous command:

```
ubuntu@ip-172-31-16-208:/opt$ spark-shell
2019-01-18 21:31:47 WARN  NativeCodeLoader:62 - Unable to load native-hadoop library for your platform... using
Setting default log level to "WARN".
To adjust logging level use sc.setLogLevel(newLevel). For SparkR, use setLogLevel(newLevel).
Spark context Web UI available at http://ip-172-31-16-208.us-east-2.compute.internal:4040
Spark context available as 'sc' (master = local[*], app id = local-1547847120337).
Spark session available as 'spark'.
Welcome to
      ____              __
     / __/__  ___ _____/ /__
    _\ \/ _ \/ _ `/ __/  '_/
   /___/ .__/\_,_/_/ /_/\_\   version 2.3.1
      /_/

Using Scala version 2.11.8 (Java HotSpot(TM) 64-Bit Server VM, Java 1.8.0_201)
Type in expressions to have them evaluated.
Type :help for more information.

scala>
```

Once the driver (one of Spark's components) is started, you can access all of the Scala and Java APIs in the shell:

1. **Spark shell for Python**: If your preferred choice of coding is Python, then you can start the Python shell of Spark with a command:

   - Add Python to Spark Path.
   - Open the `.bash_profile` and add the following lines:

     ```
     nano ~/.bash_profile

     export PYSPARK_PYTHON=python3
     export PYTHONPATH=$SPARK_HOME/python:$PYTHONPATH
     ```

   - Save the `~/.bash_profile`:

     ```
     pyspark
     ```

Once the shell has been loaded, you can start using the Python commands to access Spark APIs, as shown in the following output:

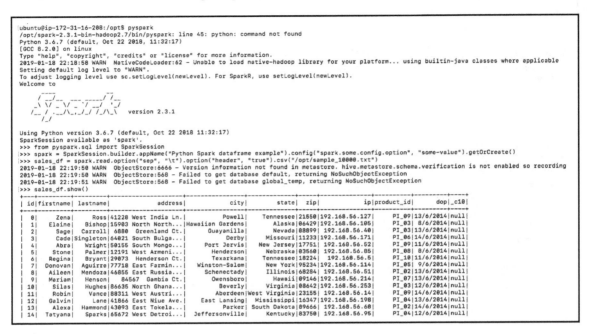

3. **Spark SQL**: If you have worked on a **relational database management system (RDBMS)** like Oracle, MySQL, or Teradata, and you want to apply your SQL programming skills to Spark, you can use the Spark SQL module to write queries for different structured datasets. To start the Spark SQL shell, all you need to do is type the following command into your machine's Terminal:

```
spark-sql
```

The following screenshot shows the set of executions that would happen when you open spark-sql. As you can see, **spark-sql** uses underlying database, which is **DERBY** by default. In Chapter 6, *Spark SQL*, you will find out how we can connect **spark-sql** to Hive metastore:

```
[ubuntu@ip-172-31-16-208:/opt$ spark-sql
2019-01-18 22:33:52 WARN  NativeCodeLoader:62 - Unable to load native-hadoop library for your platform... using builtin-java classe
2019-01-18 22:33:54 INFO  HiveMetaStore:589 - 0: Opening raw store with implemenation class:org.apache.hadoop.hive.metastore.Object
2019-01-18 22:33:54 INFO  ObjectStore:289 - ObjectStore, initialize called
2019-01-18 22:33:54 INFO  Persistence:77 - Property hive.metastore.integral.jdo.pushdown unknown - will be ignored
2019-01-18 22:33:54 INFO  Persistence:77 - Property datanucleus.cache.level2 unknown - will be ignored
2019-01-18 22:33:56 INFO  ObjectStore:370 - Setting MetaStore object pin classes with hive.metastore.cache.pinobjtypes="Table,Stora
ieldSchema,Order"
2019-01-18 22:33:59 INFO  Datastore:77 - The class "org.apache.hadoop.hive.metastore.model.MFieldSchema" is tagged as "embedded-onl
2019-01-18 22:33:59 INFO  Datastore:77 - The class "org.apache.hadoop.hive.metastore.model.MOrder" is tagged as "embedded-only" so
2019-01-18 22:33:59 INFO  Datastore:77 - The class "org.apache.hadoop.hive.metastore.model.MFieldSchema" is tagged as "embedded-onl
2019-01-18 22:33:59 INFO  Datastore:77 - The class "org.apache.hadoop.hive.metastore.model.MOrder" is tagged as "embedded-only" so
2019-01-18 22:33:59 INFO  Query:77 - Reading in results for query "org.datanucleus.store.rdbms.query.SQLQuery@0" since the connecti
2019-01-18 22:33:59 INFO  MetaStoreDirectSql:139 - Using direct SQL, underlying DB is DERBY
```

You would have a `spark-sql` shell connected to default **Derby** data store:

```
2019-01-18 22:34:02 INFO  Query:77 - Reading in results for query "org.datanucleus.store.rdbms.query.SQLQuery@0" since the connection used is closin
2019-01-18 22:34:02 INFO  MetaStoreDirectSql:139 - Using direct SQL, underlying DB is DERBY
2019-01-18 22:34:02 INFO  ObjectStore:272 - Initialized ObjectStore
2019-01-18 22:34:03 INFO  StateStoreCoordinatorRef:54 - Registered StateStoreCoordinator endpoint
spark-sql>
```

4. **Spark Submit**: The multi-lingual feature of Spark also allows you to use Java for accessing Spark APIs. Since Java (up to version 8) does not provide the REPL feature, Spark APIs are accessed and executed with the help of the following command:

```
spark-submit
```

The following syntax explains how we can specify jar with logic, the number of executors, the executor's resource specification, and the mode of execution for the application (Standalone or YARN):

```
./bin/spark-submit \
  --class <main-class> \
  --master <master-url> \
  --deploy-mode <deploy-mode> \
  --executor-memory 20G \
  --total-executor-cores 100 \
  --conf <key>=<value> \
  <application-jar> \
  [application-arguments]
```

Here, we can describe the different logic as follows:

- `--class`: This is the class containing the `main` method, and it is the entry point of the application (for example, `org.apache.spark.examples.SparkPi`).

- --master: This is the key property to define the master of your application. Depending on the standalone mode or the cluster mode, the master could be local, yarn, or spark://host:port (for example, spark://192.168.56.101:7077). More options are available at https://spark.apache.org/docs/latest/submitting-applications.html#master-urls.
- --deploy-mode: This is used to start the driver on any of worker nodes in the cluster or locally where the command is executed (client) (default: client).
- --conf: Spark configurations that you want to overwrite for your application as key=value format.
- application-jar: This is the path of your application jar. If it is present in HDFS, then you need to specify the HDFS path as hdfs:// path or if it is a file path, then it should be a valid path on a driver node, file://path.

- application-arguments: These are the arguments that you have to specify for your application's main class.

Different modes of execution

The Spark application can run in different modes, which are categorized by where and how we want to configure the master and what the executor's resource requirements are.

The master can run on the same local machine, along with executors; it can also run over a specific machine with the provided host and port. If we configure YARN as a Spark resource manager, the master can be managed by YARN:

```
# Run application locally on 8 cores
./bin/spark-submit \
 --class org.apache.spark.examples.SparkPi \
 --master local[8] \
 /path/to/examples.jar \
 100

# Run on a Spark standalone cluster in client deploy mode
./bin/spark-submit \
 --class org.apache.spark.examples.SparkPi \
 --master spark://host-ip:7077 \
 --executor-memory 20G \
 --total-executor-cores 100 \
 /path/to/examples.jar \
 1000

# Run on a YARN cluster
```

```
export HADOOP_CONF_DIR=XXX
./bin/spark-submit \
  --class org.apache.spark.examples.SparkPi \
  --master yarn \
  --deploy-mode cluster \ # can be client for client mode
  --executor-memory 20G \
  --num-executors 50 \
  /path/to/examples.jar \
  1000
```

Source: https://spark.apache.org/docs/latest/submitting-applications.html.

Spark UI: Spark provides a web interface for application execution, which is accessible by default at port **4040:** http://localhost:4040/jobs/:

Spark sandbox

To quickly start development, you can also download and configure the sandbox that's provided by Hortonworks or Cloudera. Here are the links:

- **Hortonworks:** https://hortonworks.com/tutorial/hands-on-tour-of-apache-spark-in-5-minutes/
- **Cloudera:** https://www.cloudera.com/documentation/enterprise/5-6-x/topics/quickstart.html

Summary

This chapter has helped you install Java, Scala, and Spark on a Linux machine that has been procured from an AWS EC2 instance. You can now use the same setup to execute the queries/examples that are provided in other chapters of this book.

In the next chapter, you will learn about the basic unit of Spark, which is RDD. **RDD** refers to an immutable **Resilient Distributed Dataset**, on which we can apply further actions and transformations.

3
Spark RDD

Resilient Distributed Datasets (**RDDs**) are the basic building block of a Spark application. An RDD represents a read-only collection of objects distributed across multiple machines. Spark can distribute a collection of records using an RDD and process them in parallel on different machines.

In this chapter, we shall learn about the following:

- What is an RDD?
- How do you create RDDs?
- Different operations available to work on RDDs
- Important types of RDD
- Caching an RDD
- Partitions of an RDD
- Drawbacks of using RDDs

The code examples in this chapter are written in Python and Scala only. If you wish to go through the Java and R APIs, you can visit the Spark documentation page at `https://spark.apache.org/`.

What is an RDD?

RDD is at the heart of every Spark application. Let's understand the meaning of each word in more detail:

- **Resilient**: If we look at the meaning of *resilient* in the dictionary, we can see that it means to be: *able to recover quickly from difficult conditions.* Spark RDD has the ability to recreate itself if something goes wrong. You must be wondering, *why does it need to recreate itself?* Remember how HDFS and other data stores achieve fault tolerance? Yes, these systems maintain a replica of the data on multiple machines to recover in case of failure. But, as discussed in Chapter 1, *Introduction to Apache Spark*, Spark is not a data store; Spark is an execution engine. It reads the data from source systems, transforms it, and loads it into the target system. If something goes wrong while performing any of the previous steps, we will lose the data. To provide the fault tolerance while processing, an RDD is made resilient: it can recompute itself. Each RDD maintains some information about its parent RDD and how it was created from its parent. This introduces us to the concept of **Lineage**. The information about maintaining the parent and the operation is known as lineage. Lineage can only be achieved if your data is **immutable**. What do I mean by that? If you lose the current state of an object and you are sure that previous state will never change, then you can always go back and use its past state with the same operations, and you will always recover the current state of the object. This is exactly what happens in the case of RDDs. If you are finding this difficult, don't worry! It will become clear when we look at how RDDs are created.

  Immutability also brings another advantage: *optimization.* If you know something will not change, you always have the opportunity to optimize it. If you pay close attention, all of these concepts are connected, as the following diagram illustrates:

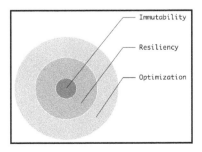

RDD

- **Distributed**: As mentioned in the following bullet point, a dataset is nothing but a collection of objects. An RDD can distribute its dataset across a set of machines, and each of these machines will be responsible for processing its *partition* of data. If you come from a Hadoop MapReduce background, you can imagine partitions as the input splits for the map phase.
- **Dataset**: A dataset is just a collection of objects. These objects can be a Scala, Java, or Python complex object; numbers; strings; rows of a database; and more.

Every Spark program boils down to an RDD. A Spark program written in Spark SQL, DataFrame, or dataset gets converted to an RDD at the time of execution.

The following diagram illustrates an **RDD** of numbers (**1** to **18**) having nine partitions on a cluster of three nodes:

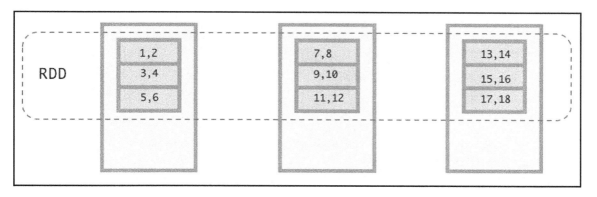

RDD

Resilient metadata

As we have discussed, apart from partitions, an RDD also stores some metadata within it. This metadata helps Spark to recompute an RDD partition in the case of failure and also provides optimizations while performing operations.

The metadata includes the following:

- A list of parent RDD dependencies
- A function to compute a partition from the list of parent RDDs
- The preferred location for the partitions
- The partitioning information, in case of pair RDDs

Right then, enough theory! Let's create a simple program and understand the concepts in more detail in the next section.

Programming using RDDs

An RDD can be created in four ways:

- **Parallelize a collection**: This is one of the easiest ways to create an RDD. You can use the existing collection from your programs, such as List, Array, or Set, as well as others, and ask Spark to distribute that collection across the cluster to process it in parallel. A collection can be distributed with the help of parallelize(), as shown here:

```
#Python
numberRDD = spark.sparkContext.parallelize(range(1,10))
numberRDD.collect()

Out[4]: [1, 2, 3, 4, 5, 6, 7, 8, 9]
```

The following code performs the same operation in Scala:

```
//scala
val numberRDD = spark.sparkContext.parallelize(1 to 10)
numberRDD.collect()

res4: Array[Int] = Array(1, 2, 3, 4, 5, 6, 7, 8, 9, 10)
```

- **From an external dataset**: Though parallelizing a collection is the easiest way to create an RDD, it is not the recommended way for the large datasets. Large datasets are generally stored on filesystems such as HDFS, and we know that Spark is built to process big data. Therefore, Spark provides a number of APIs to read data from the external datasets. One of the methods for reading external data is the textFile(). This method accepts a filename and creates an RDD, where each element of the RDD is the line of the input file.

In the following example, we first initialize a variable with the file path and then use the filePath variable as an argument of textFile() method:

```
//Scala
val filePath = "/FileStore/tables/sampleFile.log"
val logRDD = spark.sparkContext.textFile(filePath)
logRDD.collect()
```

```
res6: Array[String] = Array(2018-03-19 17:10:26 - myApp - DEBUG -
debug message 1, 2018-03-19 17:10:27 - myApp - INFO - info message
1, 2018-03-19 17:10:28 - myApp - WARNING - warn message 1,
2018-03-19 17:10:29 - myApp - ERROR - error message 1, 2018-03-19
17:10:32 - myApp - CRITICAL - critical message with some error 1,
2018-03-19 17:10:33 - myApp - INFO - info message 2, 2018-03-19
17:10:37 - myApp - WARNING - warn message, 2018-03-19 17:10:41 -
myApp - ERROR - error message 2, 2018-03-19 17:10:41 - myApp -
ERROR - error message 3)
```

If your data is present in multiple files, you can make use of `wholeTextFiles()` instead of using the `textFile()` method. The argument to `wholeTextFiles()` is the directory name that contains all the files. Each element will be represented as a key value pair, where the key will be the file name and the value will be the whole content of that file. This is useful in scenarios where you have lots of small files and want to process each file separately.

JSON and XML file are common inputs of `wholeTextFiles()` as you can parse each file separately using a parser library.

- **From another RDD**: As discussed in the first section, RDDs are immutable in nature. They cannot be modified, but we can transform an RDD to another RDD with the help of the methods provided by Spark. We shall discuss these methods in more detail in this chapter. The following example uses `filter()` to transform our `numberRDD` to `evenNumberRDD` in Python. Similarly, it also uses `filter()` to create `oddNumberRDD` in Scala:

```
#Python
evenNumberRDD = numberRDD.filter(lambda num : num%2 == 0 )
evenNumberRDD.collect()

Out[10]: [2, 4, 6, 8]
```

The following code performs the same operation in Scala:

```
//Scala
val oddNumberRDD = numberRDD.filter( num => num%2 != 0 )
oddNumberRDD.collect()

res8: Array[Int] = Array(1, 3, 5, 7, 9)
```

- **From a DataFrame or dataset**: You must be thinking, why would we ever create an RDD from a DataFrame? After all, a DataFrame is an abstraction on top of an RDD. Well, you're right! Because of this, it is advisable to use DataFrames or a dataset over an RDD, because a DataFrame brings performance benefits.

You might need to convert an RDD from a DataFrame in some scenarios where the following applies:

- The data is highly unstructured
- The data is reduced to a manageable size after heavy computations, such as joins or aggregations, and you want more control over the physical distribution of data using custom partitioning
- You have some code written in a different programming language or legacy RDD code

Let's create a DataFrame and convert it into an RDD:

```python
#Python
rangeDf = spark.range(1,5)
rangeRDD = rangeDf.rdd
rangeRDD.collect()

Out[15]: [Row(id=1), Row(id=2), Row(id=3), Row(id=4)]
```

In the preceding code, we first created a `rangeDf`DataFrame with an `id` column (the default column name) using Spark's `range()` method, which created 4 rows, from 1 to 4. We then use the `rdd` method to convert it into `rangeRDD`.

 The `range(N)` method creates values from 0 to N-1.

As we have now got a basic understanding of how to create RDDs, let's write a simple program that reads a log file and returns only the number of messages with log levels of `ERROR` and `INFO`:

```
$ cat sampleFile.log
2018-03-19 17:10:26 - myApp - DEBUG - debug message 1
2018-03-19 17:10:27 - myApp - INFO - info message 1
2018-03-19 17:10:28 - myApp - WARNING - warn message 1
2018-03-19 17:10:29 - myApp - ERROR - error message 1
2018-03-19 17:10:32 - myApp - CRITICAL - critical message with some error 1
2018-03-19 17:10:33 - myApp - INFO - info message 2
2018-03-19 17:10:37 - myApp - WARNING - warn message
```

```
2018-03-19 17:10:41 - myApp - ERROR - error message 2
2018-03-19 17:10:41 - myApp - ERROR - error message 3
```

The preceding code shows the content of the sampleFile.log files. Each line in sampleFile.log represents a log with its log level.

The next code snippets calculates the number of ERROR and INFO messages in the log file using the Python API:

```
#Python
filePath = "/FileStore/tables/sampleFile.log"

logRDD = spark.sparkContext.textFile(filePath)

resultRDD = logRDD.filter(lambda line : line.split(" - ")[2] in
['INFO','ERROR'])\
                    .map(lambda line : (line.split(" - ")[2], 1))\
                    .reduceByKey(lambda x, y : x + y)

resultRDD.collect()


Out[27]: [('INFO', 2), ('ERROR', 3)]
```

The following code performs the same operation in Scala:

```
//Scala
val filePath = "/FileStore/table/sampleFile.log"

val logRDD = spark.sparkContext.textFile(filePath)

val resultRDD = logRDD.filter(line =>
Array("INFO","ERROR").contains(line.split(" -")(2)))
  .map(line => (line.split(" - ")(2), 1))
  .reduceByKey( _ + _ )

resultRDD.collect()


res12: Array[(String, Int)] = Array((ERROR,3), (INFO,2))
```

In the preceding two examples, we first created a `filePath` variable that contained the path to our log file. We then made use of the `textFile()` method to create our base RDD, that is `logRDD`. Under the hood, Spark adds this operation into its DAG. At the time of execution, Spark will read our `sampleFile.log` and distribute it to multiple executors. In the next line, we make use of `filter()` to get only those lines that have `"INFO"` and `"ERROR"` as the log level. The `filter()` method accepts a function as input and returns a Boolean. We also pipe the output of `filter` to a `map()` object, and now the problem is reduced to the word-count problem. At this point, `map()` will only receive the filtered lines and assign 1 to each record. We aggregate the records based on the log level using `reduceByKey()`, which adds all the values for each log level. We finally collect our result using the `collect()` method. This is the point where Spark actually starts executing the DAG.

Transformations and actions

We have discussed some basic operations for creating and manipulating RDDs. Now it is time to categorize them into two main categories:

- Transformations
- Actions

Transformation

As the name suggests, transformations help us in transforming existing RDDs. As an output, they always create a new RDD that gets computed lazily. In the previous examples, we have discussed many transformations, such as `map()`, `filter()`, and `reduceByKey()`.

Transformations are of two types:

- Narrow transformations
- Wide transformations

Narrow transformations

Narrow transformations transform data without any shuffle involved. These transformations transform the data on a per-partition basis; that is to say, each element of the output RDD can be computed without involving any elements from different partitions. This leads to an important point: The new RDD will always have the same number of partitions as its parent RDDs, and that's why they are easy to recompute in the case of failure. Let's understand this with the following example:

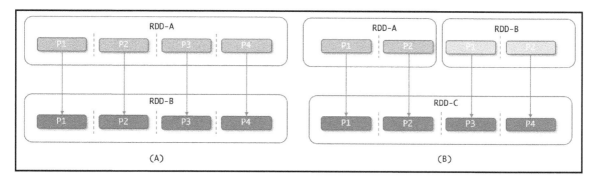

Narrow transformations

So, we have an **RDD-A** and we perform a narrow transformation, such as `map()` or `filter()`, and we get a new **RDD-B** with the same number of partitions as **RDD-A**. In part **(B)**, we have two, **RDD-A** and **RDD-B**, and we perform another type of narrow transformation such as `union()`, and we get a new **RDD-C** with the number of partitions equal to the sum of partitions of its parent RDDs (**A** and **B**). Let's look at some examples of narrow transformations.

map()

This applies a given function to each element of an RDD and returns a new RDD with the same number of elements. For example, in the following code, numbers from 1 to 10 are multiplied by the number 2:

```Python
#Python
spark.sparkContext.parallelize(range(1,11)).map(lambda x : x * 2).collect()
```

The following code performs the same operation in Scala:

```
//Scala
spark.sparkContext.parallelize(1 to 10).map(_ * 2).collect()
```

flatMap()

This applies a given function that returns an iterator to each element of an RDD and returns a new RDD with more elements. In some cases, you might need multiple elements from a single element. For example, in the following code, an RDD containing lines is converted into another RDD containing words:

```
#Python
spark.sparkContext.parallelize(["It's fun to learn Spark","This is a
flatMap example using Python"]).flatMap(lambda x : x.split(" ")).collect()
```

The following code performs the same operation in Scala:

```
//Scala
spark.sparkContext.parallelize(Array("It's fun to learn Spark","This is a
flatMap example using Python")).flatMap(x => x.split(" ")).collect()
```

filter()

The `filter()` transformation applies a function that filters out the elements that do not pass the condition criteria, as shown in the following code. For example, if we need numbers greater than 5, we can pass this condition to the `filter()` transformation. Let's create an RDD of numbers 1 to 10 and filter out numbers that are greater than 5:

```
#Python
spark.sparkContext.parallelize(range(1,11)).filter(lambda x : x >
5).collect()
```

The following code performs the same operation in Scala:

```
//Scala
spark.sparkContext.parallelize(1 to 10).filter(_ > 5).collect()
```

Any function that returns a Boolean value can be used used to filter out the elements.

union()

The `union()` transformation takes another RDD as an input and produces a new RDD containing elements from both the RDDs, as shown in the following code. Let's create two RDDs: one with numbers 1 to 5 and another with numbers 5 to 10, and then concatenate them together to get a new RDD with the numbers 1 to 10:

```python
#Python
firstRDD = spark.sparkContext.parallelize(range(1,6))
secordRDD = spark.sparkContext.parallelize(range(5,11))
firstRDD.union(secordRDD).collect()
```

The following code performs the same operation in Scala:

```scala
//scala
val firstRDD = spark.sparkContext.parallelize(1 to 5)
val secordRDD = spark.sparkContext.parallelize(5 to 10)
firstRDD.union(secordRDD).collect()
```

The `union()` transformation does not remove duplicates. If you are coming from a SQL background, `union()` performs the same operation as `Union All` in SQL.

mapPartitions()

The `mapPartitions()` transformation is similar to `map()`. It also allows users to manipulate elements of an RDD, but it provides more control at a per-partition basis. It applies a function that accepts an iterator as an argument and returns an iterator as the output. If you have done some shell scripting and you are aware of **AWK** programming, then you can correlate that with `mapPartitions` transformation to understand it better. A typical AWK example looks something like `BEGIN { #Begin block } { #middle block } END { #end Block }`. The `Begin` block executes only once before reading the file content, the `middle` block executes for each line in the input file, and the `end` block also executes only once at the end of the file. Similarly, if you want some operations to be performed at the beginning or end of processing all elements one by one, you can make use of the `mapPartitions()` transformation. In the following code, we are multiplying each element by 2, but this time with `mapPartitions()`:

```python
#Python
spark.sparkContext.parallelize(range(1,11), 2).mapPartitions(lambda
iterOfElements : [e*2 for e in iterOfElements]).collect()
```

The following code performs the same operation in Scala:

```scala
//scala
spark.sparkContext.parallelize(1 to 10, 2).mapPartitions(iterOfElements =>
for (e <- iterOfElements) yield e*2 ).collect()
```

One example where you might use `mapPartitions()` is when you need to open a
database connection at the beginning of each partition.

 If you want to create an object only once and want that object to be used
during computation in each partition, you can make use of `broadcast`
variables.

Wide transformations

Wide transformations involve a shuffle of the data between the partitions.
The `groupByKey()`, `reduceByKey()`, `join()`, `distinct()`, and `intersect()` are some
examples of wide transformations. In the case of these transformations, the result will be
computed using data from multiple partitions and thus requires a shuffle. Wide
transformations are similar to the shuffle-and-sort phase of MapReduce. Let's understand
the concept with the help of the following example:

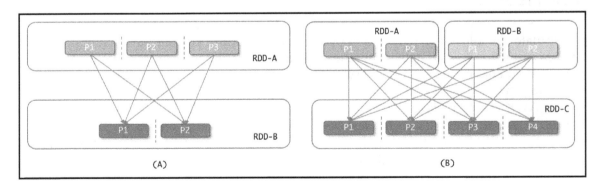

Wide transformations

We have an **RDD-A** and we perform a wide transformation such as `groupByKey()` and we
get a new **RDD-B** with fewer partitions. **RDD-B** will have data grouped by each key in the
dataset. In part **(B)**, we have two RDDs: **RDD-A**, and **RDD-B** and we perform another type
of wide transformation such as `join()` or `intersection()` and get a new **RDD-C**. The
following are some examples of wide transformations.

distinct()

The `distinct()` transformation removes duplicate elements and returns a new RDD with unique elements as shown. Let's create an RDD with some duplicate elements (1, 2, 3, 4) and use `distinct()` to get an RDD with unique numbers:

```Python
#Python
spark.sparkContext.parallelize([1,1,2,2,3,3,4,4]).distinct().collect()
```

The following code performs the same operation in Scala:

```scala
//scala
spark.sparkContext.parallelize(Array(1,1,2,2,3,3,4,4)).distinct().collect()
```

sortBy()

We can sort an RDD with the help of `sortBy()` transformation. It accepts a function that can be used to sort the RDD elements. In the following example, we sort our RDD in descending order using the second element of the tuple:

```Python
#Python
spark.sparkContext.parallelize([('Rahul', 4),('Aman', 2),('Shrey',
6),('Akash', 1)]).sortBy(lambda x : -x[1]).collect()
```

The following code performs the same operation in Scala:

```scala
//scala
spark.sparkContext.parallelize(Array(("Rahul", 4),("Aman", 2),("Shrey",
6),("Akash", 1))).sortBy( _._2 * -1 ).collect()
```

The previous code will result in this:

```
[('Shrey', 6), ('Rahul', 4), ('Aman', 2), ('Akash', 1)]
```

intersection()

The `intersection()` transformation allows us to find common elements between two RDDs. Like `union()` transformation, `intersection()` is also a set operation between two RDDs, but involves a shuffle. The following examples show how to find common elements between two RDDs using `intersection()`:

```Python
#Python
firstRDD = spark.sparkContext.parallelize(range(1,6))
secordRDD = spark.sparkContext.parallelize(range(5,11))
firstRDD.intersection(secordRDD).collect()
```

The following code performs the same operation in Scala:

```scala
//Scala
val firstRDD = spark.sparkContext.parallelize(1 to 5)
val secordRDD = spark.sparkContext.parallelize(5 to 10)
firstRDD.intersection(secordRDD).collect()
```

The previous code gives a result of 5.

subtract()

You can use subtract() transformation to remove the content of one RDD using another RDD. Let's create two RDDs: The first one has numbers from 1 to 10 and the second one has elements from 6 to 10. If we use subtract(), we get a new RDD with numbers 1 to 5:

```python
#Python
firstRDD = spark.sparkContext.parallelize(range(1,11))
secordRDD = spark.sparkContext.parallelize(range(6,11))
firstRDD.subtract(secordRDD).collect()
```

The following code performs the same operation in Scala:

```scala
//scala
val firstRDD = spark.sparkContext.parallelize(1 to 10)
val secordRDD = spark.sparkContext.parallelize(6 to 10)
firstRDD.subtract(secordRDD).collect()
```

In the previous example, we have two RDDs: firstRDD contains elements from 1 to 10 and secondRDD contains elements 6 to 10. After applying the subtract() transformation, we get a new RDD containing elements from 1 to 5.

cartesian()

The cartesian() transformation can join elements of one RDD with all the elements of another RDD and results in the cartesian product of two. In the following examples, firstRDD has elements [0, 1, 2] and secondRDD has elements ['A', 'B', 'C']. We use cartesian() to get the cartesian product of two RDDs:

```python
#Python
firstRDD = spark.sparkContext.parallelize(range(3))
secordRDD = spark.sparkContext.parallelize(['A','B','C'])
firstRDD.cartesian(secordRDD).collect()
```

The following code performs the same operation in Scala:

```scala
//scala
val firstRDD = spark.sparkContext.parallelize(0 to 2)
val secordRDD = spark.sparkContext.parallelize(Array("A","B","C"))
firstRDD.cartesian(secordRDD).collect()
```

Here is the output from the previous example:

```scala
//Scala
Array[(Int, String)] = Array((0,A), (0,B), (0,C), (1,A), (1,B), (1,C),
(2,A), (2,B), (2,C))
```

Remember these operations involve a shuffle, and therefore require lots of computing resources such as memory, disk, and network bandwidth.

 `textFile()` and `wholeTextFiles()` are also considered transformations, as they create a new RDD from external data.

Action

You would have noticed that in every example we used, the `collect()` method to get the output. To get the final result back to the driver, Spark provides another type of operation known as *actions*. At the time of transformations, Spark chains these operations and constructs a DAG, but nothing gets executed. Once an action is performed on an RDD, it forces the evaluation of all the transformations required to compute that RDD.

Actions do not create a new RDD. They are used for the following:

- Returning final results to the driver
- Writing final result to an external storage
- Performing some operation on each element of that RDD (for example, `foreach()`)

Let's discuss some of the basic actions.

collect()

The `collect()` action returns all the elements of an RDD to the driver program. You should only use `collect()` if you are sure about the size of your final output. If the size of the final output is huge, then your driver program might crash while receiving the data from the executors. The use of `collect()` is not advised in production. The following example collects all the elements of an RDD containing numbers from 0 to 9:

```
#Python
spark.sparkContext.parallelize(range(10)).collect()

Out[26]: [0, 1, 2, 3, 4, 5, 6, 7, 8, 9]
```

count()

Use `count()` to count the number of elements in the RDD. The following Scala code counts the number of an RDD and returns 10 as output:

```
//scala
spark.sparkContext.parallelize(1 to 10).count()

res17: Long = 10
```

take()

The `take()` action returns *N* number of elements from an RDD. The following code returns the first two elements from an RDD containing the numbers 0 to 9:

```
#Python
spark.sparkContext.parallelize(range(10)).take(2)

Out[27]: [0, 1]
```

top()

The `top()` action returns the top *N* elements from the RDD. The following code returns the top 2 elements from an RDD:

```
#Python
spark.sparkContext.parallelize(range(10)).top(2)

Out[28]: [9, 8]
```

takeOrdered()

If you want to get *N* element based on an ordering, you can use a `takeOrdered()` action. You can also make use of `sortBy()` transformation, followed by a `take()` action. Both approaches trigger a data shuffle. In the following example, we take out 3 elements from the RDD, containing numbers from 0 to 9, by providing our own sorting criteria:

```python
#Python
spark.sparkContext.parallelize(range(10)).takeOrdered(3, key = lambda x: -x)

Out[3]: [9, 8, 7]
```

Here, we took the first 3 elements in decreasing order.

first()

The `first()` action returns the first element of the RDD. The following example returns the first element of the RDD:

```python
#Python
spark.sparkContext.parallelize(range(10)).first()

Out[4]: 0
```

countByValue()

The `countByValue()` action can be used to find out the occurrence of each element in the RDD. The following is the Scala code that returns a `Map` of key-value pair. In the output, `Map`, the key is the RDD element, and the value is the number of occurrences of that element in the RDD:

```scala
//Scala
spark.sparkContext.parallelize(Array("A","A","B","C")).countByValue()

res0: scala.collection.Map[String,Long] = Map(A -> 2, B -> 1, C -> 1)
```

reduce()

The `reduce()` action combines the RDD elements in parallel and gives aggregated results as output. In the following example, we calculate the sum of the first 10 natural numbers:

```Scala
//Scala
spark.sparkContext.parallelize(1 to 10).reduce( _ + _ )

res1: Int = 55
```

saveAsTextFile()

To save the results to an external data store, we can make use of `saveAsTextFile()` to save your result in a directory. You can also specify a compression codec to store your data in compressed form. Let's write our number RDD to a file:

```Python
#Python
spark.sparkContext.parallelize(range(10)).saveAsTextFile('/FileStore/tables
/result')
```

In the preceding example, we provide a directory as an argument, and Spark writes data inside this directory in multiple files, along with the success file (`_success`).

 If an existing directory is provided as an argument to, `saveAsTextFile()` action, then the job will fail with the `FileAlreadyExistsException` exception. This behavior is important because we might rewrite a directory accidentally that holds data from a heavy job.

foreach()

The `foreach()` function applies a function to each element of the RDD. The following example concatenates the string `Mr.` to each element using `foreach()`:

```Scala
//Scala
spark.sparkContext.parallelize(Array("Smith","John","Brown","Dave")).foreac
h{ x => println("Mr. "+x) }
```

If you run the previous example in local mode, you will see the output. But, in the case of cluster mode, you won't be able to see the results, because `foreach()` performs the given function inside the executors and does not return any data to the driver.

This is mainly used to work with accumulators. We shall see this in more detail in `Chapter` `5`, *Spark Architecture and Application Execution Flow*.

You can find more transformations and actions at `https://spark.apache.org/docs/2.3.` `0/rdd-programming-guide.html#transformations`.

Types of RDDs

RDDs can be categorized in multiple categories. Some of the examples include the following:

Hadoop RDD	Shuffled RDD	Pair RDD
Mapped RDD	Union RDD	JSON RDD
Filtered RDD	Double RDD	Vertex RDD

We will not discuss all of them in this chapter, as it is outside the scope of this chapter. But we will discuss one of the important types of RDD: **pair RDDs**.

Pair RDDs

A pair RDD is a special type of RDD that processes data in the form of key-value pairs. Pair RDD is very useful because it enables basic functionalities such as `join` and `aggregations`. Spark provides some special operations on these RDDs in an optimized way. If we recall the examples where we calculated the number of `INFO` and `ERROR` messages in `sampleFile.log` using `reduceByKey()`, we can clearly see the importance of the pair RDD.

One of the ways to create a pair RDD is to parallelize a collection that contains elements in the form of `Tuple`. Let's look at some of the transformations provided by a pair RDD.

groupByKey()

Elements having the same key can be grouped together with the help of a `groupByKey()` transformation. The following example aggregates data for each key:

```Python
#Python
pairRDD = spark.sparkContext.parallelize([(1, 5),(1, 10),(2, 4),(3, 1),(2, 6)])
result = pairRDD.groupByKey().collect()
for pair in result:
```

```
    print 'key -',pair[0],', value -', list(pair[1])
```

```
Output:
key - 1 , value - [5, 10]
key - 2 , value - [4, 6]
key - 3 , value - [1]
```

The following code performs the same operation in Scala:

```scala
//Scala
val pairRDD = spark.sparkContext.parallelize(Array((1, 5),(1, 10),(2,
4),(3, 1),(2, 6)))
val result = pairRDD.groupByKey().collect()
result.foreach {
  pair => println("key - "+pair._1+", value -"+pair._2.toList)
}
```

```
Output:
key - 1, value -List(5, 10)
key - 2, value -List(4, 6)
key - 3, value -List(1)
```

The groupByKey() transformation is a wide transformation that shuffles data between executors based on the key. An important point here is to note that groupByKey() does not aggregate data, it only groups is based on the key. The groupByKey() transformation should be used with the caution. If you understand your data really well, then groupByKey() can bring some advantages in some scenarios. For example, let's assume you have a key-value data, where the key is the country code and value is the transaction amount, and your data is highly skewed based on the fact that more than 90% of your customers are based in the USA. In this case, if you use groupByKey() to group your data, then you might face some issues because Spark will shuffle all the data and try to send records with the USA to a single machine. This might result in a failure. There are some techniques such as **salted keys** to avoid such scenarios.

Despite this drawback, groupByKey can be very useful in some scenarios. If you know your data is not skewed and you want to compute multiple aggregations such as max, min, and average using the same underlying data, then you can first group the elements using groupByKey() and persist it.

reduceByKey()

A `reduceByKey()` transformation is available on Pair RDD. It allows aggregation of data by minimizing the data shuffle and performs operations on each key in parallel. A `reduceByKey()` transformation first performs the local aggregation within the executor and then shuffles the aggregated data between each node. In the following example, we calculate the sum for each key using `reduceByKey`:

```Python
#Python
pairRDD = spark.sparkContext.parallelize([(1, 5),(1, 10),(2, 4),(3, 1),(2, 6)])
pairRDD.reduceByKey(lambda x,y : x+y).collect()

Output:
[(1, 15), (2, 10), (3, 1)]
```

The following code performs the same operation in Scala:

```Scala
//Scala
val pairRDD = spark.sparkContext.parallelize(Array((1, 5),(1, 10),(2, 4),(3, 1),(2, 6)))
pairRDD.reduceByKey(_+_).collect()

Output:
Array[(Int, Int)] = Array((1,15), (2,10), (3,1))
```

A `reduceByKey()` transformation can only be used for associative aggregations, for example: $(A+B) + C = A + (B+C)$.

sortByKey()

The `sortByKey()` can be used to sort the pair RDD based on keys. In the following example, we first create an RDD by parallelizing a list of tuples and then sort it by the first element of the tuple:

```Python
#Python
pairRDD = spark.sparkContext.parallelize([(1, 5),(1, 10),(2, 4),(3, 1),(2, 6)])
pairRDD.sortByKey().collect()

Output:
[(1, 5), (1, 10), (2, 4), (2, 6), (3, 1)]
```

By default, `sortByKey()` sorts elements in ascending order, but you can change the sorting order by passing your custom ordering. For example, `sortByKey(keyfunc =lambda k: -k)` will sort the RDD in descending order.

join()

The `join()` transformation will join two pair RDDs based on their keys. The following example joins data based on the country and returns only the matching records:

```scala
//Scala
val salesRDD = spark.sparkContext.parallelize(Array(("US",20),("IND",
30),("UK",10)))
val revenueRDD = spark.sparkContext.parallelize(Array(("US",200),("IND",
300)))

salesRDD.join(revenueRDD).collect()

Output:
Array[(String, (Int, Int))] = Array((US,(20,200)), (IND,(30,300)))
```

There are some more transformations available on pair RDD such as `aggregateByKey()`, `cogroup()`, `leftOuterJoin()`, `rightOuterJoin()`, `subtractByKey()`, and more. Some of the special actions include `countByKey()`, `collectAsMap()`, and `lookup()`.

Caching and checkpointing

Caching and checkpointing are some of the important features of Spark. These operations can improve the performance of your Spark jobs significantly.

Caching

Caching data into memory is one of the main features of Spark. You can cache large datasets in-memory or on-disk depending upon your cluster hardware. You can choose to cache your data in two scenarios:

- Use the same RDD multiple times
- Avoid reoccupation of an RDD that involves heavy computation, such as `join()` and `groupByKey()`

If you want to run multiple actions of an RDD, then it will be a good idea to cache it into the memory so that recompilation of this RDD can be avoided. For example, the following code first takes out a few elements from the RDD and then returns the count of the elements:

```scala
//Scala
val baseRDD = spark.sparkContext.parallelize(1 to 10)
baseRDD.take(2)
baseRDD.count()
```

The following code makes use of `cache()` to make the application efficient:

```scala
//Scala
val baseRDD = spark.sparkContext.parallelize(1 to 10)
baseRDD.cache() //Caching baseRDD
baseRDD.take(2)
baseRDD.count()
```

Spark will compute `baseRDD` twice to perform `take()` and `count()` actions. We cache our `baseRDD` and then run the actions. This computes the RDD only once and performs the action on top of cached data. In this example, there might not be much difference in the performance, as here we are dealing with very small datasets. But you can imagine the bottleneck in the case of big data.

Spark does not cache the data immediately as soon as we write the `cache()` operation. But it makes a note of this operation, and once it encounters the first action, it will compute the RDD and cache it based on the caching level.

The following table lists multiple data persistence levels provided by Spark:

Level	Definition
MEMORY_ONLY	Stores data in memory as unserialized Java objects
MEMORY_ONLY_SER	Stores data in memory but as serialized Java objects
MEMORY_AND_DISK	Unserialized Java objects in memory and remaining serialized data on disk
MEMORY_AND_DISK_SER	Serialized Java objects in memory plus remaining serialized data on disk
DISK_ONLY	Stores data on disk
OFF_HEAP	Stores serialized RDD off-heap in Techyon (Spark's in-memory storage)

You can replicate the cached data on two nodes by writing _2 at the end of the persisting level.

One important point to note here is that in the case of the MEMORY_ONLY caching level, if some of the data doesn't fit into the memory, the remaining data is not stored inside the disk by default. The remaining partitions are recomputed at the time of execution. Cache is not a transformation nor an action.

> It is recommended to unpersist your cached RDDs once you have finished with that RDD. You can call unpersist(), which removes the data from memory.

Checkpointing

The life cycle of the cached RDD will end when the Spark session ends. If you have computed an RDD and you want it to use in another Spark program without recomputing it, then you can make use of the checkpoint() operation. This allows storing the RDD content on the disk, which can be used for the later operations. Let's discuss this with the help of an example:

```python
#Python
baseRDD = spark.sparkContext.parallelize(['A','B','C'])
spark.sparkContext.setCheckpointDir("/FileStore/tables/checkpointing")
baseRDD.checkpoint()
```

We first create a baseRDD and set a checkpointing directory using setCheckpointDir() method. Finally, we store the content of baseRDD using checkpoint().

Understanding partitions

Data partitioning plays a really important role in distributed computing, as it defines the degree of parallelism for the applications. Understating and defining partitions in the right way can significantly improve the performance of Spark jobs. There are two ways to control the degree of parallelism for RDD operations:

- repartition() and coalesce()
- partitionBy()

repartition() versus coalesce()

Partitions of an existing RDD can be changed using `repartition()` or `coalesce()`. These operations can redistribute the RDD based on the number of partitions provided.

The `repartition()` can be used to increase or decrease the number of partitions, but it involves heavy data shuffling across the cluster. On the other hand, `coalesce()` can be used only to decrease the number of partitions. In most of the cases, `coalesce()` does not trigger a shuffle. The `coalesce()` can be used soon after heavy filtering to optimize the execution time. It is important to notice that `coalesce()` does not always avoid shuffling. If the number of partitions provided is much smaller than the number of available nodes in the cluster then data will be shuffled across some node, but `coalesce()` will still give a better performance than `repartition()`. The following diagram shows the difference between `repartition()` and `coalesce()`:

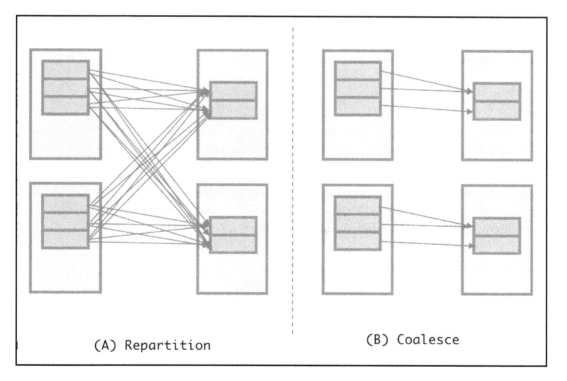

(A) Repartition   (B) Coalesce

Repartition and Coalesce

The `repartition()` is not that bad after all. In some cases, when your job is not using all the available slots, you can repartition your data to run it faster.

partitionBy()

Any operation that shuffles the data accepts an additional parameter, that is, degrees of parallelism. This allows users to provide the number of partitions for the produced RDD. The following example shows how you can change the number of partitions of the new RDD by passing an additional parameter:

```scala
//Scala
val baseRDD = spark.sparkContext.parallelize(Array(("US",20),("IND",
30),("UK",10)), 3)
println(baseRDD.getNumPartitions)

Output:
3
```

The following code changes the number of partitions of the new RDD:

```scala
//Scala
val groupedRDD = baseRDD.groupByKey(2)
println(groupedRDD.getNumPartitions)

Output:
2
```

The `baseRDD` has 3 partitions. We have passed an additional parameter to `groupByKey` which will tell Spark to produce `groupedRDD` with 2 partitions.

Spark also provides `partitionBy()` operation, which can be used to control the number of partitions. A partitioning function can be passed as an argument to `partitionBy()` to redistribute the data of an RDD. This is quite useful in some operations, such as `join()`. Let's understand this with the help of an example:

```scala
//Scala
import org.apache.spark.HashPartitioner

val baseRDD = spark.sparkContext.parallelize(Array(("US",20),("IND",
30),("UK",10)), 3)
baseRDD.partitionBy(new HashPartitioner(2)).persist()
```

This shows the usage of `partitionBy()`. We have passed a `HashPartitioner()` that will redistribute the data based on the key values and create two partitions of `baseRDD`. Spark can take advantage of this information and minimize the data shuffle during the `join()` transformation.

It is advisable to persist the RDD after repartitioning if the RDD is going to be used frequently.

Drawbacks of using RDDs

An RDD is a compile-time type-safe. That means, in the case of Scala and Java, if an operation is performed on the RDD that is not applicable to the underlying data type, then Spark will give a compile time error. This can avoid failures in production.

There are some drawbacks of using RDDs though:

- RDD code can sometimes be very opaque. Developers might struggle to find out what exactly the code is trying to compute.
- RDDs cannot be optimized by Spark, as Spark cannot look inside the lambda functions and optimize the operations. In some cases, where a `filter()` is piped after a wide transformation, Spark will never perform the filter first before the wide transformation, such as `reduceByKey()` or `groupByKey()`.
- RDDs are slower on non-JVM languages such as Python and R. In the case of these languages, a Python/R virtual machine is created alongside JVM. There is always a data transfer involved between these VMs, which can significantly increase the execution time.

Summary

In this chapter, we first learned about the basic idea of an RDD. We then looked at how we can create RDDs using different approaches, such as creating an RDD from an existing RDD, from an external data store, from parallelizing a collection, and from a DataFrame and datasets. We also looked at the different types of transformations and actions available on RDDs. Then, the different types of RDDs were discussed, especially the pair RDD. We also discussed the benefits of caching and checkpointing in Spark applications, and then we learned about the partitions in more detail, and how we can make use of features like partitioning, to optimize our Spark jobs.

In the end, we also discussed some of the drawbacks of using RDDs. In the next chapter, we'll discuss the DataFrame and dataset APIs and see how they can overcome these challenges.

4
Spark DataFrame and Dataset

In the previous chapter, we learned about RDD concepts and APIs. In this chapter, we will explore DataFrame APIs, which are abstractions over RDDs, and also discuss the dataset APIs that come with Spark 2.0 to provide various optimizations over DataFrames.

The following topics will be covered in this chapter:

- DataFrames
- Datasets

DataFrames

As we already mentioned, DataFrame APIs are abstractions of RDD APIs. DataFrames are distributed collections of data that are organized in the form of rows and columns. In other words, DataFrames provide APIs to efficiently process structured data that's available in different sources. The sources could be an RDD, different types of files in a filesystem, any RDBMS, or Hive tables.

The features of DataFrames are as follows:

- DataFrames can process data that's available in different formats, such as CSV, AVRO, and JSON, or stored in any storage media, such as Hive, HDFS, and RDBMS
- DataFrames can process data volumes from kilobytes to petabytes
- Use the Spark-SQL query optimizer to process data in a distributed and optimized manner
- Support for APIs in multiple languages, including Java, Scala, Python, and R

Creating DataFrames

To start with, we need a **Spark session object**, which will be used to convert RDDs into DataFrames, or to load data directly from a file into a DataFrame.

We are using the sales dataset in this chapter. You can get the dataset file, along with the code files for this chapter, from the following link: https://github.com/PacktPublishing/Apache-Spark-Quick-Start-Guide:

```scala
//Scala
import org.apache.spark.sql.SparkSession
val spark = SparkSession.builder().appName("Spark DataFrame
example").config("spark.some.config.option", "value").getOrCreate()
// For implicit conversions like converting RDDs to DataFrames
import spark.implicits._
```

```java
//Java
import org.apache.spark.sql.SparkSession;
SparkSession spark = SparkSession.builder().appName("Java Spark DataFrame
example").config("spark.some.config.option", "value").getOrCreate();
```

```python
#Python
from pyspark.sql import SparkSession
spark = SparkSession.builder.appName("Python Spark DataFrame
example").config("spark.some.config.option", "value").getOrCreate()
```

Source: https://spark.apache.org/docs/latest/sql-programming-guide.html#starting-point-sparksession.

Once the spark session has been created in the language of your choice, you can either convert an RDD into a DataFrame or load data from any file storage in to a DataFrame:

```scala
//Scala
val sales_df = spark.read.option("sep", "\t").option("header",
"true").csv("file:///opt/data/sales/sample_10000.txt")
// Displays the content of the DataFrame to stdout
sales_df.show()
```

```java
//Java
import org.apache.spark.sql.Dataset;
import org.apache.spark.sql.Row;
Dataset<Row> df_sales = spark.read.option("sep", "\t").option("header",
"true").csv("file:///opt/data/sales/sample_10000.txt");
// Displays the content of the DataFrame to stdout
sales_df.show()
```

```Python
#Python
sales_df = spark.read.option("sep", "\t").option("header",
"true").csv("file:///opt/data/sales/sample_10000.txt")
# Displays the content of the DataFrame to stdout
sales_df.show()
```

For files in HDFS and S3, the filepath format will have `hdfs://` or `S3://` instead of `file://`.

If files do not have header information in them, you can skip the (`header`, `true`) option.

Data sources

Spark SQL allows users to query a wide variety of data sources. These sources could be files, such as **Java Database Connectivity** (**JDBC**).

There are a couple of ways to load data. Let's take a look at both methods:

- Load data from `parquet`:

```Scala
//Scala
val sales_df = spark.read.option("sep", "\t").option("header",
"true").csv("file:///opt/data/sales/sample_10000.txt")

sales_df.write.parquet("sales.parquet")

val parquet_sales_DF = spark.read.parquet("sales.parquet")
parquet_sales_DF.createOrReplaceTempView("parquetSales")

val ipDF = spark.sql("SELECT ip FROM parquetSales WHERE id BETWEEN
10 AND 19")
ipDF.map(attributes => "IPS: " + attributes(0)).show()
```

```Java
//Java
import org.apache.spark.sql.Dataset;
import org.apache.spark.sql.Row;
Dataset<Row> df_sales = spark.read.option("sep",
"\t").option("header",
"true").csv("file:///opt/data/sales/sample_10000.txt");

// Write data to parquet file
df_sales.write().parquet("sales.parquet");

// Parquet preserve the schema of file
```

```java
Dataset<Row> parquetSalesDF =
spark.read().parquet("sales.parquet");

parquetSalesDF.createOrReplaceTempView("parquetSales");
Dataset<Row> ipDF = spark.sql("SELECT ip FROM parquetSales WHERE id
BETWEEN 10 AND 19");
Dataset<String> ipDS = ipDF.map(
    (MapFunction<Row, String>) row -> "IP: " + row.getString(0),
    Encoders.STRING());
ipDS.show();
```

```python
#Python
sales_df = spark.read.option("sep", "\t").option("header",
"true").csv("file:///opt/data/sales/sample_10000.txt")

sales_df.write.parquet("sales.parquet")

parquetSales = spark.read.parquet("sales.parquet")

parquetSales.createOrReplaceTempView("parquetSales")
ip = spark.sql("SELECT ip FROM parquetsales WHERE id >= 10 AND id
<= 19")
ip.show()
```

- Load data from JSON:

```scala
//Scala
val sales_df = spark.read.option("sep", "\t").option("header",
"true").csv("file:///opt/data/sales/sample_10000.txt")

sales_df.write.json("sales.json")

val json_sales_DF = spark.read.json("sales.json")
json_sales_DF.createOrReplaceTempView("jsonSales")

var ipDF = spark.sql("SELECT ip FROM jsonSales WHERE id BETWEEN 10
AND 19")
ipDF.map(attributes => "IPS: " + attributes(0)).show()
```

DataFrame operations and associated functions

DataFrames support *untyped transformations* with the following operations:

- `printSchema`: This prints out the mapping for a Spark DataFrame in a tree structure. The following code will give you a clear idea of how this operation works:

```scala
//Scala
import spark.implicits._
// Print the schema in a tree format
sales_df.printSchema()
```

```java
//Java
import static org.apache.spark.sql.functions.col;

// Print the schema in a tree format
sales_df.printSchema();
```

```python
#Python
# Print the schema in a tree format
sales_df.printSchema()
```

The output you get should look like this:

```
scala> sales_df.printSchema()
root
 |-- id: string (nullable = true)
 |-- firstname: string (nullable = true)
 |-- lastname: string (nullable = true)
 |-- address: string (nullable = true)
 |-- city: string (nullable = true)
 |-- state: string (nullable = true)
 |-- zip: string (nullable = true)
 |-- ip: string (nullable = true)
 |-- product_id: string (nullable = true)
 |-- date_of_purchase: string (nullable = true)
```

- `select`: This allows you to select a set of columns from a DataFrame. The following code will give you a clear idea of how this operation works:

```scala
//Scala
import spark.implicits._
sales_df.select("firstname").show()
```

```java
//Java
import static org.apache.spark.sql.functions.col;
sales_df.select("firstname").show()
```

```
#Python
sales_df.select("firstname").show()
```

The output you get should look like this:

```
scala> sales_df.select("firstname").show()
+---------+
|firstname|
+---------+
|     Zena|
|   Elaine|
|     Sage|
|     Cade|
|     Abra|
|    Stone|
|   Regina|
|  Donovan|
|   Aileen|
|   Mariam|
|    Silas|
|    Robin|
|   Galvin|
|    Alexa|
|  Tatyana|
|     Yuri|
|     Raya|
|  Ulysses|
|   Edward|
|  Emerald|
+---------+
only showing top 20 rows
```

- filter: This allows you to filter rows from a DataFrame based on certain conditions. The following code will give you a clear idea of how this operation works:

```
//Scala
import spark.implicits._
sales_df.filter($"id" < 50).show()
```

```
//Java
import static org.apache.spark.sql.functions.col;
sales_df.filter(col("id").gt(9990)).show();
```

```
#Python
sales_df.filter(sales_df['id'] < 50).show()
```

The output you get should look like this:

```
scala> sales_df.filter($"id" < 15).show()
+---+---------+---------+--------------------+----------------+-------------+-----+--------------+----------+----------------+
| id|firstname| lastname|             address|            city|        state|  zip|            ip|product_id|date_of_purchase|
+---+---------+---------+--------------------+----------------+-------------+-----+--------------+----------+----------------+
|  0|     Zena|     Ross|41228 West India Ln.|          Powell|    Tennessee|21550|192.168.56.127|     PI_09|       13/6/2014|
|  1|   Elaine|   Bishop|15903 North North...| Hawaiian Gardens|       Alaska|06429|192.168.56.105|     PI_03|        8/6/2014|
|  2|     Sage|  Carroll| 6880  Greenland Ct.|       Guayanilla|       Nevada|08899| 192.168.56.40|     PI_03|       13/6/2014|
|  3|     Cade|Singleton|64021 South Bulga...|           Derby|     Missouri|11233|192.168.56.171|     PI_06|       14/6/2014|
|  4|     Abra|   Wright|50155 South Mongo...|    Port Jervis|   New Jersey|17751| 192.168.56.52|     PI_09|       11/6/2014|
|  5|    Stone|   Palmer|12191 West Armeni...|       Henderson|     Nebraska|03560| 192.168.56.85|     PI_08|        8/6/2014|
|  6|   Regina|   Bryant|29073  Henderson Ct.|       Texarkana|    Tennessee|18224|  192.168.56.5|     PI_10|       11/6/2014|
|  7|  Donovan|  Aguirre|77718 East Farmin...|   Winston-Salem|     New York|95234|192.168.56.114|     PI_05|        9/6/2014|
|  8|   Aileen|   Mendoza|46855 East Russia...|     Schenectady|     Illinois|68284| 192.168.56.51|     PI_02|       13/6/2014|
|  9|   Mariam|   Henson|  84567  Gambia Ct.|       Owensboro|       Hawaii|09146|192.168.56.214|     PI_07|       13/6/2014|
| 10|    Silas|   Hughes|86635 North Ghana...|         Beverly|     Virginia|08642|192.168.56.253|     PI_03|       12/6/2014|
| 11|    Robin|    Vance|88311 West Austri...|        Aberdeen|West Virginia|23155| 192.168.56.14|     PI_09|       14/6/2014|
| 12|   Galvin|     Lane|41866 East Niue Ave.|    East Lansing|  Mississippi|16347|192.168.56.198|     PI_04|       13/6/2014|
| 13|    Alexa|  Hammond|43093 East Tokela...|          Parker| South Dakota|89666| 192.168.56.68|     PI_02|       14/6/2014|
| 14|  Tatyana|   Sparks|65672 West Detroi...| Jeffersonville|     Kentucky|83750|  192.168.56.95|     PI_04|       12/6/2014|
+---+---------+---------+--------------------+----------------+-------------+-----+--------------+----------+----------------+
```

- groupBy: This allows you to group rows in a DataFrame based on a set of columns, and apply aggregated functions such as count(), avg(), and so on on the grouped dataset. The following code will give you a clear idea of how this operation works:

```scala
//Scala
import spark.implicits._
sales_df.groupBy("ip").count().show()
```

```java
//Java
import static org.apache.spark.sql.functions.col;
sales_df.groupBy("ip").count().show();
```

```python
#Python
sales_df.groupBy("ip").count().show()
```

The output you get should look like this:

```
scala> sales_df.groupBy("ip").count().show()
+--------------+-----+
|            ip|count|
+--------------+-----+
|192.168.56.141|   35|
| 192.168.56.30|   41|
|192.168.56.129|   36|
| 192.168.56.91|   39|
| 192.168.56.36|   40|
|192.168.56.170|   46|
|192.168.56.173|   44|
| 192.168.56.54|   45|
|192.168.56.100|   32|
| 192.168.56.70|   35|
|192.168.56.190|   39|
|  192.168.56.7|   33|
|192.168.56.119|   40|
| 192.168.56.34|   29|
| 192.168.56.56|   39|
| 192.168.56.57|   49|
|192.168.56.104|   42|
| 192.168.56.15|   41|
| 192.168.56.13|   36|
|192.168.56.216|   47|
+--------------+-----+
only showing top 20 rows
```

A complete list of DataFrame functions that can be used with these operations is available here:

`https://spark.apache.org/docs/latest/api/scala/index.html#org.apache.spark.sql.functions$`.

Running SQL on DataFrames

Other than DataFrame operations and functions, DataFrames also allow you to run SQL directly on data. For this, all we need to do is create temporary views on DataFrames. These views are categorized as local or global views.

Temporary views on DataFrames

This feature enables developers to run SQL queries in a program, and get the result as a DataFrame:

```scala
//Scala
sales_df.createOrReplaceTempView("sales")
```

```
val sqlDF = spark.sql("SELECT * FROM sales")
sqlDF.show()

//Java
import org.apache.spark.sql.Dataset;
import org.apache.spark.sql.Row;
sales_df.createOrReplaceTempView("sales");
Dataset<Row> sqlDF = spark.sql("SELECT * FROM sales");
sqlDF.show();

#Python
sales_df.createOrReplaceTempView("sales")
sqlDF = spark.sql("SELECT * FROM sales")
sqlDF.show()
```

Global temporary views on DataFrames

Temporary views only last for the session in which they are created. If we want to have views available across various sessions, we need to create **Global Temporary Views**. The view definition is stored in the default database, `global_temp`. Once a view is created, we need to use the fully qualified name to access it in a query:

```
//Scala
sales_df.createGlobalTempView("sales")
// Global temporary view is tied to a system database `global_temp`
spark.sql("SELECT * FROM global_temp.sales").show()
spark.newSession().sql("SELECT * FROM global_temp.sales").show()

//Java
sales_df.createGlobalTempView("sales");
spark.sql("SELECT * FROM global_temp.sales").show();
spark.newSession().sql("SELECT * FROM global_temp.sales").show();

#Python
sales_df.createGlobalTempView("sales")
# Global temporary view is tied to a system database `global_temp`
spark.sql("SELECT * FROM global_temp.sales").show()
spark.newSession().sql("SELECT * FROM global_temp.sales").show()
```

Datasets

Datasets are strongly typed collections of objects. These objects are usually domain-specific and can be transformed in parallel using relational or functional operations.

These operations are further categorized into actions and transformations. Transformations are functions that generate new datasets, while actions compute datasets and return the transformed results. Transformation functions include Map, FlatMap, Filter, Select, and Aggregate, while Action functions include count, show, and save to any filesystem.

The following instructions will help you create a dataset from a CSV file:

1. Initialize SparkSession:

```scala
//Scala
import org.apache.spark.sql.SparkSession
val spark = SparkSession.builder().appName("Spark DataSet
example").config("spark.config.option", "value").getOrCreate()
// For implicit conversions like converting RDDs to DataFrames
import spark.implicits._
```

```java
//Java
import org.apache.spark.sql.SparkSession;
SparkSession spark = SparkSession.builder().appName("Java Spark
DataFrame example").config("spark.config.option",
"value").getOrCreate();
```

```python
#Python
from pyspark.sql import SparkSession
spark = SparkSession.builder.appName("Python Spark DataFrame
example").config("spark.config.option", "value").getOrCreate()
```

2. Define an encoder for this CSV:

```
case class Sales (id: Int, firstname: String,lastname:
String,address: String,city: String,state: String,zip: String,ip:
String,product_id: String,date_of_purchase: String)
```

3. Load the dataset from the CSV with type sales:

```scala
//Scala
import org.apache.spark.sql.types._
import org.apache.spark.sql.Encoders
val sales_ds = spark.read.option("sep", "\t").option("header",
"true").csv("file:///opt/data/sales/sample_10000.txt").withColumn("
id", 'id.cast(IntegerType)).as[Sales]
```

```
// Displays the content of the Dataset to stdout
sales_ds.show()

//Java
import org.apache.spark.sql.Dataset;
import org.apache.spark.sql.Row;
Dataset<Row> sales_ds = spark.read.option("sep",
"\t").option("header",
"true").csv("file:///opt/data/sales/sample_10000.txt");
// Displays the content of the Dataset to stdout
sales_ds.show()

#Python
sales_ds = spark.read.option("sep", "\t").option("header",
"true").csv("file:///opt/data/sales/sample_10000.txt")
# Displays the content of the Dataset to stdout
sales_ds.show()
```

The following image shows how we can create a **Dataset** of **Sales** CSV data, along with a **Sales** encoder defined for a dataset:

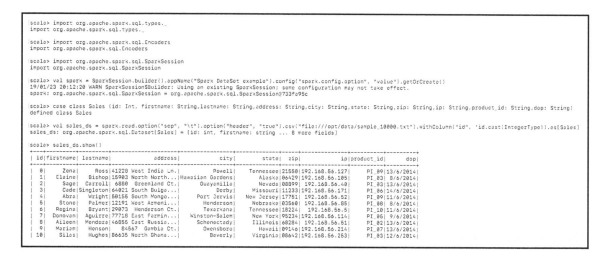

Important differences in a dataset compared to DataFrames are as follows:

- Defining a case class to define types of columns in CSV
- If the interpreter takes up a different type by inference, we need to cast to the exact type using the `withColumn` property
- The output is a dataset of `Type Sales`, not a DataFrame

We need to check the correctness of the data, as it is possible that the actual data does not match with the Type defined. There are three options to deal with this situation:

1. Permissive: This is the default mode in which, if the data type is not matched with the schema type, the data fields are replaced with null:

```
val sales_ds = spark.read.option("sep", "\t").option("header",
"true").option("mode",
"PERMISSIVE").csv("file:///opt/data/sales/sample_10000.txt").withCo
lumn("id", 'id.cast(IntegerType)).as[Sales]
```

2. DROPMALFORMED: As the name suggests, this mode will drop records where the parser finds a mismatch between the data type and schema type:

```
val sales_ds = spark.read.option("sep", "\t").option("header",
"true").option("mode",
"DROPMALFORMED").csv("file:///opt/data/sales/sample_10000.txt").wit
hColumn("id", 'id.cast(IntegerType)).as[Sales]
```

3. FAILFAST: This mode will abort further processing on the first mismatch between data type and schema type:

```
val sales_ds = spark.read.option("sep", "\t").option("header",
"true").option("mode",
"FAILFAST").csv("file:///opt/data/sales/sample_10000.txt").withColu
mn("id", 'id.cast(IntegerType)).as[Sales]
```

Datasets work on the concept of *lazy evaluation*, which means for every transformation, a new dataset definition is created, but no execution happens at the backend. In this case, it only creates a logical plan that describes the computation flow required to execute the transformation. The actual evaluation happens once we have an action being called on the dataset. With an action, the Spark query optimizer optimizes the logical plan and creates a physical plan of execution. This physical plan then computes the datasets in a parallel and distributed way. The explain function is used to check for the logical and optimized physical plan.

The following image shows the explain plan for the **sales** dataset:

```
10  // Loading dataset from CSV
11  import org.apache.spark.sql.types._
12  import org.apache.spark.sql.Encoders
13  var sales_ds = spark.read.option("sep", "\t").option("header", "true").csv("/FileStore/tables/sample_10000.txt").withColumn("id",
    'id.cast(IntegerType)).as[Sales]
14  // Displays the content of the Dataset to stdout
15  sales_ds.explain
```

```
▼ (1) Spark Jobs
  ▶ Job 219  View (Stages: 1/1)

== Physical Plan ==
*(1) Project [cast(id#6994 as int) AS id#7016, firstname#6995, lastname#6996, address#6997, city#6998, state#6999, zip#7000, ip#7001, product_id#70
02, dop#7003, _c10#7004]
+- *(1) FileScan csv [id#6994,firstname#6995,lastname#6996,address#6997,city#6998,state#6999,zip#7000,ip#7001,product_id#7002,dop#7003,_c10#7004] B
atched: false, DataFilters: [], Format: CSV, Location: InMemoryFileIndex[dbfs:/FileStore/tables/sample_10000.txt], PartitionFilters: [], PushedFilt
ers: [], ReadSchema: struct<id:string,firstname:string,lastname:string,address:string,city:string,state:string,zip:str...
import org.apache.spark.sql.SparkSession
spark: org.apache.spark.sql.SparkSession = org.apache.spark.sql.SparkSession@55983c90
import spark.implicits._
defined class Sales
import org.apache.spark.sql.types._
import org.apache.spark.sql.Encoders
sales_ds: org.apache.spark.sql.Dataset[Sales] = [id: int, firstname: string ... 9 more fields]
```

Encoders

Encoders are required to map domain-specific objects of type `T` to Spark's type system or internal Spark SQL representation. An `Encoder` of type `T` is a trait represented by `Encoder[T]`.

Encoders are available with every Spark session, and you can explicitly import them with spark `implicits` as `import spark.implicits._`.

For example, given an `Employee` class with the fields name (`String`) and salary (`int`), an encoder is used as an indicator to serialize the `Employee` object to binary form. This binary structure provides the following advantages:

- Occupies less memory
- Data is stored in columnar format for efficient processing

Let's take a look at the major encoder features:

- **Fast serialization:** Encoders are used for runtime code with custom bytecode generation for serialization and deserialization. These are significantly faster than Java and Kryo serializers. Along with faster serialization, encoders also provide significant data compression, which helps with better network transfers. Encoders produce data in Tungsten binary format, which also allows different operations in place, rather than materializing data to an object.

- **Support for semi-structured data:** Encoders allow Spark to process complex JSON with type-safe Scala and Java.

Let's look at an example. Consider the following `sales` dataset in JSON structure, or use the previous commands to write the JSON file from a CSV file:

```
{"id": "1", "firstname": "Elaine", "lastname": "Bishop","address": "15903
North North Adams Blvd.", "city": "Hawaiian Gardens", "state":
"Alaska","zip": "06429", "ip": "192.168.56.105", "product_id": "PI_03",
"dop":"8/6/2018"}

{"id": "2", "firstname": "Sage", "lastname": "Carroll","address": "6880
Greenland Ct.", "city": "Guayanilla", "state": "Nevada","zip": "08899",
"ip": "192.168.56.40", "product_id": "PI_04", "dop":"13/6/2018"}
```

To convert JSON data fields into a type, we can define a `case class` with a structure and `map` input data in to the defined structure. Columns in the `case class` are mapped to keys in JSON, and types are mapped as defined in the `case class`:

```
case class Sales(id: String,firstname: String,lastname: String,address:
String,city: String,state: String,zip: String,ip: String,product_id:
String,dop: String )

val sales = sqlContext.read.json("sales.json").as[Sales]

sales.map(s => s"${s.firstname} purchased product ${s.product_id} on
${s.dop}")
```

Encoders also check the type of the expected schema with data, and give an error in the case of any type mismatch. For example, if we define a byte type in a class where the encoder finds more integers, it will complain instead of processing TBs of data with auto casting integers to byte and losing precision:

```
case class Sales(id: byte)

val sales= sqlContext.read.json("sales.json").as[Sales]
```

```
org.apache.spark.sql.AnalysisException: Cannot upcast id
from int to smallint as it may truncate
```

Encoders can also handle complex types, including arrays and maps.

Internal row

Encoders are coded as **traits** in Spark 2.0. They can be thought of as an efficient means of serialization/deserialization for Spark SQL 2.0, similar to **SerDes** in Hive:

```
trait Encoder[T] extends Serializable {
  def schema: StructType
  def clsTag: ClassTag[T]
}
```

Encoders internally convert type T to Spark SQL's InternalRow type, which is the binary row representation.

Creating custom encoders

Encoders can be created based on Java and Kryo serializers. Encoder factory objects are available in the org.apache.spark.sql package:

```
import org.apache.spark.sql.Encoders

// Normal Encoder
scala> Encoders.LONG
res1: org.apache.spark.sql.Encoder[Long] = class[value[0]: bigint]

// Kryo and Java Serialization Encoders
case class Sales(id: String, firstname: String, product_id: Boolean)

scala> Encoders.kryo[Sales]
res3: org.apache.spark.sql.Encoder[Sales] = class[value[0]: binary]

scala> Encoders.javaSerialization[Sales]
res5: org.apache.spark.sql.Encoder[Sales] = class[value[0]: binary]

// Scala tuple encoders
scala> Encoders.tuple(Encoders.scalaLong, Encoders.STRING,
Encoders.scalaBoolean)
res9: org.apache.spark.sql.Encoder[(Long, String, Boolean)] = class[_1[0]:
bigint, _2[0]: string, _3[0]: boolean]
```

Summary

In this chapter, we started by loading a dataset into a DataFrame, and then applying different transformations to the DataFrame. Later, we went through the latest additions of dataset APIs and encoders in Spark 2.0.

In the next chapter, we will go through Spark's architecture and its components in detail. We will also see, in detail, the flow of a Spark application once it is submitted.

5

Spark Architecture and Application Execution Flow

So far in this book, we have discussed how you can create your own Spark application using RDDs and the DataFrame and dataset APIs. We also discussed some basic concepts of Spark, such as transformations, actions, caching, and repartitions, which enable you to write your Spark applications efficiently. In this chapter, we'll discuss what happens under the hood when you run your Spark application. We'll also walk you through the different tools and techniques available for monitoring your jobs. This chapter will discuss the following:

- Spark components and their respective roles in the application execution
- The life cycle of a Spark application
- Monitoring Spark applications

A sample application

To better understand the life cycle of the Spark application, let's create a sample application and understand the execution step by step. The following example shows the content of the data file that we will use in our application. The `sale.csv` file stores information,such as `PRODUCT_CODE`, `COUNTRY_CODE`, and the order `AMOUNT` for each `ORDER_ID`:

```
$ cat sale.csv

ORDER_ID,PRODUCT_CODE,COUNTRY_CODE,AMOUNT
1,PC_01,USA,200.00
2,PC_01,USA,46.34
3,PC_04,USA,123.54
4,PC_02,IND,99.76
5,PC_44,IND,245.00
6,PC_02,AUS,654.21
7,PC_03,USA,75.00
```

```
8,PC_01,SPN,355.00
9,PC_03,USA,34.02
10,PC_03,USA,567.07
```

We shall now create a sample application using Python API to find out the total sales amount by country and sort them in descending order by the total amount. The following example shows the code of our sample application:

```
from pyspark.sql import SparkSession
from pyspark.sql.functions import desc

spark = SparkSession.Builder().appName('Sales Application').getOrCreate()

sales_df = spark.read \
      .option("inferSchema", "true") \
      .option("header", "true") \
      .csv("/user/data/sales.csv")

result = sales_df.groupBy("COUNTRY_CODE")\
                .sum("AMOUNT")\
                .orderBy(desc("sum(AMOUNT)"))

result.show()
```

In the previous example, we first imported `SparkSession` from the `pyspark.sql`, along with the function `desc()` from the `functions` module. In Scala, `SparkSession` can be found inside the `org.apache.spark.sql` package. `SparkSession` is primarily responsible for two main things:

- Initializing a Spark cluster, that is, Drivers and Executors
- Communicating with the cluster manager for job submission and status updates

In the earlier version of Spark (1.x), there are two separate contexts:`SparkContext` and `SQLContext`. In Spark 2.x, they have been combined under a single context,`SparkSession`.

The first step is to create our `SparkSession` by assigning it an application name and storing it in a `spark` variable. We then load the sales data from `sale.csv`, available on **Hadoop Distributed Files System(HDFS)**, into the `sales_df` DataFrame. If you want Spark to read a file from the local filesystem, you can specify the file path with `file:///`. We use `.option()` to infer the schema for `sales_df` DataFrame. Next, we write our logic to aggregate the sales data by `COUNTRY_CODE` and calculate the total sales for each country. Finally, we run a `show()` action to trigger the computation. Now, we need package our application in `example.py` in order to submit it to Spark. We shall use `spark-submit` utility provided by Spark to submit our job. The following example shows how we submit our application in a YARN cluster:

```
$ spark-submit \
  --master yarn
  --deploy-mode client
  --num-executors 3
  --executor-memory 2g \
  --total-executor-cores 1 \
  example.py
```

As discussed earlier in this book, Spark integrates well with a variety of cluster managers such as YARN, Mesos, and Kubernetes. In our example, we are running our application on YARN. We set the cluster manager using `--master` option of `spark-submit`. Flags such as `--num-executors`, `--executor-memory`, and `--total-executor-cores` are used to provide the resource requirements to the cluster manager. We'll explain the use of `--deploy-mode` flag shortly.

The following is the output of our sales application:

```
+------------+-----------+
|COUNTRY_CODE|sum(AMOUNT)|
+------------+-----------+
| USA        | 1045.97   |
| AUS        | 654.21    |
| SPN        | 355.0     |
| IND        | 344.76    |
+------------+-----------+
```

When we submit our application, SparkSession inside Spark's driver communicates with the YARN resource manager to allocate resources and initialize the executors on the worker machines. The following diagram shows the states of the **YARN Cluster**, Spark Driver, and executors. The cluster consists of a **Cluster Manager Node** and two worker nodes. We have submitted our job from the **Client Node**. These machines are also called the **gateway** or **edge** nodes. Our driver process is running on the client node and executors (**E1, E2,** and **E3**) are running on **Cluster Worker Node**. All executors register themselves with the **Driver** program to provide a complete view of the Spark cluster:

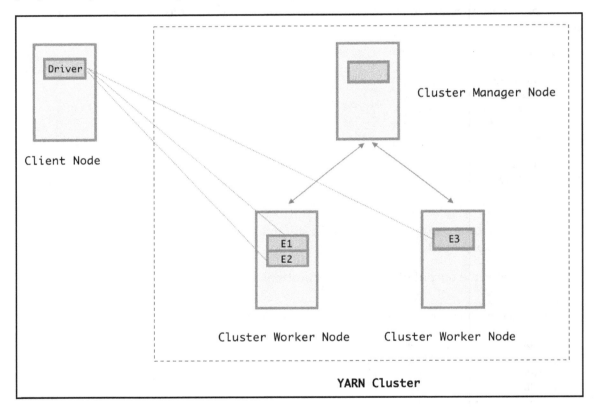

spark-submit in client mode

A Spark job is submitted automatically when Spark encounters an action (in our case, show()). This means a Spark application can have more than one job based on the number of actions. Spark driver will now call the scheduler, which has two main parts:

- DAG constructor
- Task scheduler

DAG constructor

The **DAG constructor** is responsible for breaking down a *job* into a set of *stages*.

Stage

A **stage** is nothing but a group of tasks that Spark can execute together without involving a shuffle.A stage boundary is decided based on the nature of transformations we use in our applications. In Chapter 3, *Spark RDD*, we discussed wide transformations and narrow transformations. Wide transformations are the ones that shuffle the data across a network, such as groupByKey, Join, and Distinct. These transformations decide the number of stages in a Spark job. In our example.py file, we are using groupBy() transformation to find out the total amount by each country and orderBy() to order the data by total amount, and therefore we should have three stages for our job. We can view the stage information using an explain() operation on an RDD or a DataFrame. The following shows the output of explain() on our result DataFrame. We can see that there are three stages in total:

```
result.explain()

== Physical Plan ==
*(3) Sort [sum(AMOUNT)#345 DESC NULLS LAST], true, 0
+- Exchange rangepartitioning(sum(AMOUNT)#345 DESC NULLS LAST, 200)
   +- *(2) HashAggregate(keys=[COUNTRY_CODE#313],
functions=[sum(AMOUNT#314)])
      +- Exchange hashpartitioning(COUNTRY_CODE#313, 200)
         +- *(1) HashAggregate(keys=[COUNTRY_CODE#313],
functions=[partial_sum(AMOUNT#314)])
            +- *(1) FileScan csv [COUNTRY_CODE#313,AMOUNT#314] Batched:
false, Format: CSV, Location:
InMemoryFileIndex[file:/Users/agrade/Akash/Work/Python/sales.csv],
PartitionFilters: [], PushedFilters: [], ReadSchema:
struct<COUNTRY_CODE:string,AMOUNT:double>
```

Earlier, we saw the DAG of stages for our sample application in graphical form. In the following DAG, the first stage (**Stage 1**) corresponds to reading the data from `sale.csv` and then triggering some shuffle (**exchange**) tasks. The second stage (**Stage 2**) performs the aggregation, and finally, the third stage (**Stage 3**) results in an ordered list of country codes and their respective total amounts:

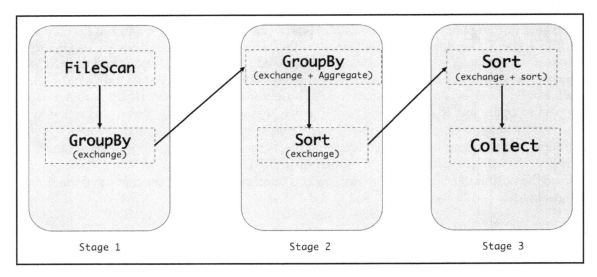

Stages

Tasks

We will now discuss an important concept: **tasks**. Each stage consists of a set of tasks. A task is a composition of a data partition and a set of transformations. As shown earlier, these tasks can be piped together in a stage. Tasks are of two types:

- **Shuffle map tasks**: Shuffle map tasks are like the map-side tasks of a MapReduce program. They perform the transformation and create a new partition of data.
- **Result tasks**: These are tasks performed by operations, such as `show()`, to return the results back to the users.

It is important to understand these concepts to write efficient applications, because it may have a significant effect on your jobs. For example, if you are processing a large single partition, then you will only have one task running and you will lose on the parallelism. On the other hand, if you process a large number of small partitions, then you will have as many tasks as the number of partitions. That is why choosing the right number of partitions is the key for better performance.

Task scheduler

It is the responsibility of the task scheduler to schedule these tasks with an executor based on the available cores and data locality. By default, a task is assigned a single core to perform its operation. You can change this behavior by configuring `spark.task.cpus` property. Spark provides two choices for scheduling policies:

- **First in-First out (FIFO)**
- **FAIR**

FIFO

FIFO is the default scheduling policy provided by Spark. It is okay to use FIFO when you are in the learning phase, but it is not ideal for production applications. In the case of FIFO, when the jobs are submitted, their tasks execute in the order they arrive. This means, if you have a stage running on a Spark cluster that is occupying half of the resources, then another stage can execute its task on available resources. But, sometimes, this becomes a problem. If the first stage is a heavy one and consumes all the available resources, then the second stage will not be able to execute its tasks.

FAIR

FAIR scheduling is an alternate to FIFO. This policy offers equal resources to all the tasks in **round robin** fashion. For example, when the first task is assigned the resources, it is only assigned one portion of the resources. The second task will be assigned the next portion of the resources, and so on. One of the advantages is to restrict long-lived applications to consume all the available resources.

You can change the default policy by setting the `spark.scheduler.mode` property:

```
spark.conf.set("spark.scheduler.mode","FAIR")
```

Application execution modes

When it comes to running your application, you'll need to decide how your job is going to run. In the previous section, when we submitted our job from the client node, our driver process was running on the same machine and executors running on the cluster worker nodes. Spark is not restricted to only this mode of execution. It provides three execution modes:

- Local mode
- Client mode
- Cluster mode

In this section, we'll discuss each of them in detail and how you can use `spark-submit` to configure them.

Local mode

Local mode runs both driver and executors on a single machine. In this mode, the partitions are processed by multiple threads in parallel. The number of threads can be controlled by the user while submitting the job. This mode is useful in the learning phase but, not recommended for production applications, as you only use a single machine to process the data.

The following shows how you can submit a job in local mode with `spark-submit`:

```
$ spark-submit --master local example.py
```

Client mode

In the **client mode**, the driver process runs on the client node (that is, the edge or gateway node) on which the job was submitted. The client node provides resources, such as memory, CPU, and disk space to the driver program, but the executors run on the cluster nodes and they are maintained by the cluster manager, such as YARN. Earlier, we saw how we used client mode to submit our sales application in the previous section. One of the advantages of running your job in client mode is that you can easily access your logs on the same machine. But when your number of Spark applications increase in production, you should not consider client mode for job execution. This is because the client node has limited resources. If some of the applications collect data from executors, there is a high chance of client node failure.

As shown here, we use the `--deploy-mode` parameter from `spark-submit` to specify the client mode:

```
$ spark-submit \
    --master yarn
    --deploy-mode client
    --num-executors 3
    --executor-memory 2g \
    --total-executor-cores 1 \
    example.py
```

Cluster mode

Cluster mode is similar to client mode, except that the driver process runs on one of the cluster worker machines, and the cluster manager is responsible for both driver and executor processes. This gives an advantage of running multiple applications at the same time because cluster manager will distribute the driver load across the cluster. This mode is the most common and recommended mode for running the Spark applications. In this mode, the logs can be collected from the cluster manager or you can implement a central logging solution to gather the application logs.

The following diagram shows our sale application running in cluster mode. **Driver** process is running on the first worker node and all executors are running on different worker nodes:

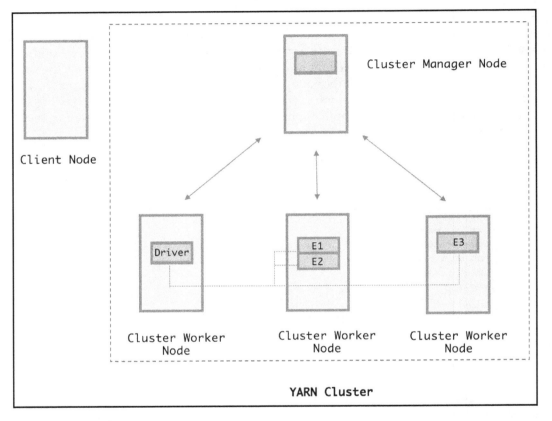

Cluster mode

The following example code shows how you can submit a job in cluster mode with spark-submit:

```
$ spark-submit \
    --master yarn
    --deploy-mode cluster
    --num-executors 3
    --executor-memory 2g \
    --total-executor-cores 1 \
    example.py
```

The following table shows all the possible options available for `--master` in `spark-submit`:

Master URL	Meaning
`local`	Run Spark locally with one worker thread (that is, no parallelism at all).
`local[K]`	Run Spark locally with K worker threads (ideally, set this to the number of cores on your machine).
`local[K,F]`	Run Spark locally with K worker threads and F `maxFailures` (see `spark.task.maxFailures` for an explanation of this variable).
`local[*]`	Run Spark locally with as many worker threads as logical cores on your machine.
`local[*,F]`	Run Spark locally with as many worker threads as logical cores on your machine and F `maxFailures`.
`spark://HOST:PORT`	Connect to the given `Spark standalone cluster` master. The port must be whichever one your master is configured to use, which is 7077 by default.
`spark://HOST1:PORT1,HOST2:PORT2`	Connect to the given `Spark standalone cluster with standby masters with Zookeeper`. The list must have all the master hosts in the high availability cluster set up with Zookeeper. The port must be whichever each master is configured to use, which is 7077 by default.
`mesos://HOST:PORT`	Connect to the given `Mesos` cluster. The port must be whichever one your application is configured to use, which is 5050 by default. Or, for a Mesos cluster using ZooKeeper, use `mesos://zk://....` To submit with `--deploy-mode cluster`, the HOST:PORT should be configured to connect to the `MesosClusterDispatcher`.
`yarn`	Connect to a `YARN`cluster in client or cluster mode depending on the value of `--deploy-mode`. The cluster location will be found based on the `HADOOP_CONF_DIR` or `YARN_CONF_DIR` variable.
`k8s://HOST:PORT`	Connect to a `Kubernetes` cluster in cluster mode. Client mode is currently unsupported and will be supported in future releases. The HOST and PORT refer to the [Kubernetes API Server](`https://kubernetes.io/docs/reference/generated/kube-apiserver/`). It connects using TLS by default. To force it to use an unsecured connection, you can use `k8s://http://HOST:PORT`.

More information can be found at `https://spark.apache.org/docs/latest/submitting-applications.html`.

Application monitoring

This section covers a different way of monitoring your Spark application. It is important to monitor your jobs to get a better understanding of your application's behavior. These observations can help you optimize your application code. There are different ways you can monitor your jobs.

Spark UI

Spark provides a built-in monitoring UI that provides useful information about your Spark applications. When you submit your job, Spark launches this UI at the driver host on the default port, 4040. If port 4040 is not available, then Spark tries to bind it on the next available port. You can also change this default setting by changing `spark.ui.port` property. Spark UI has multiple tabs:

- **Jobs**: Provides information such as DAG, Stages, Tasks, and duration about your Spark jobs
- **Stages**: Provides information about all the stages in details
- **Storage**: Provides information about cached partitions
- **Environment**: Information about the execution environment, such as `spark.scheduler.mode`, can be viewed here
- **Executors**: This tab shows information about each executor
- **SQL**: Provides information about the structured APIs (SQL, DataFrame, and dataset)

Following image shows a sample Spark UI showing details about a Spark job:

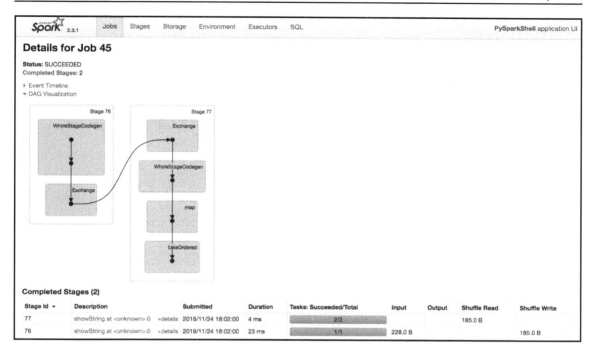

Spark UI

Application logs

An alternate way to monitor your Spark application is through the application logs. You can use logging libraries (`logging` in Python; `log4j` in Java/Scala) available in the different languages to log the events to get a better understanding of your application.

External monitoring solution

You can also integrate your application logging with a central logging system such as Graphite, Ganglia, Splunk, **Elasticsearch, Logstash, and Kibana (ELK)**, or Prometheus. These systems provide you the flexibility to query your log data or even create custom dashboards.

Summary

In this chapter, we discussed the life cycle of the Spark application, Spark components, and their roles in job execution. We first created a sample application in Python and used `spark-submit` to run our application. We discussed how the driver process constructs the DAG and its stages, and how tasks are scheduled on a cluster. In addition, we also discussed different execution modes offered by Spark in detail. Finally, we discussed possible ways to monitor your application.

In the next chapter, we shall discuss Spark SQL in detail.

6
Spark SQL

In our previous chapter, we learned about DataFrames and datasets and how we can use or write custom encoders to have type-safe operations on datasets. This chapter explains the SQL component of Spark, which helps developers working on Hive or familiar with RDBMS SQL to use a similar style in Spark.

We will be covering the following topics in this chapter:

- Spark metastore
- SQL language manual
- SQL database using **Java Database Connectivity** (**JDBC**)

Spark SQL

Spark SQL is an abstraction of data using **SchemaRDD**, which allows you to define datasets with schema and then query datasets using SQL. To start with, you just have to type `spark-sql` in the Terminal with Spark installed. This will open a Spark shell for you.

Spark metastore

To store databases, table names, and schema, Spark installs a default database, `metastore.db`, at the same location from where you started the SQL shell.

Using the Hive metastore in Spark SQL

Spark provides the flexibility to leverage the existing Hive metastore. This will allow users to access table definitions as available to Hive in Spark and to run the same HiveQL in Spark. The difference will be that queries running on Spark will be executed as per the Spark execution plan, and underlying data will be processed as per Spark execution and optimizations. These queries wont follow the MapReduce path, which is the default in Hive.

For many queries, users can see a tremendous performance gain with the Spark execution engine compared to the MapReduce engine, due to the optimized plan of execution in Spark.

Hive configuration with Spark

Hive on Spark gives Hive the capacity to use Apache as its execution motor. We will be using the following steps to configure Hive:

1. Copy `hive-site.xml` to the Spark configuration folder as follows:

   ```
   cp $HIVE_HOME/conf/hive-site.xml $SPARK_HOME/conf/
   ```

2. Add the following line to `~/.bash_profile`:

   ```
   export SPARK_CLASSPATH=$HIVE_HOME/lib/mysql-connector-java-3.1.14-bin.jar

   source ~/.bash_profile
   ```

3. Run the following command to access Spark SQL:

   ```
   spark-sql
   ```

Check for existing databases and tables with the `Show Databases` and `Show Tables` commands. You'll find all of the databases and corresponding tables that you have in Hive.

SQL language manual

Spark SQL provides a set of **Data Definition Languages** (DDLs) and **Data Manipulation Languages** (DMLs). These are the same as, or very similar to, Hive and other basic SQL language specifications.

Database

In this section, we will be looking at some operations that we can perform on a database:

1. Create Database: We will be using the following command to create a database:

   Create Database if not exists mydb
   location '/opt/sparkdb';

   The output following execution will be similar to this:

   ```
   [spark-sql> show databases;
   default
   Time taken: 2.584 seconds, Fetched 1 row(s)
   spark-sql> Create Database if not exists mydb
   [         > location '/opt/sparkdb';
   chgrp: changing ownership of 'file:///opt/sparkdb': chown:
   Time taken: 0.342 seconds
   [spark-sql> show databases;
   default
   mydb
   Time taken: 0.061 seconds, Fetched 2 row(s)
   spark-sql> █
   ```

2. Describe Database: We will be using the following command to describe a database:

   Describe Database [extended] mydb;

   The output after execution will be similar to this:

   ```
   [spark-sql> Describe Database mydb;
   Database Name    mydb
   Description
   Location         file:/opt/sparkdb
   Time taken: 0.089 seconds, Fetched 3 row(s)
   [spark-sql> Describe Database Extended mydb;
   Database Name    mydb
   Description
   Location         file:/opt/sparkdb
   Properties
   Time taken: 0.063 seconds, Fetched 4 row(s)
   ```

3. SHOW DATABASES: We will be using the following command to display a database:

```
SHOW DATABASES [LIKE 'pattern']
```

pattern could be any partial search string or *.

4. use mydb: The following command can be given to use a database:

```
use mydb;
```

5. DROP DATABASE: We will be using the following command to describe a database:

```
DROP DATABASE [IF EXISTS] mydb [(RESTRICT|CASCADE)]
```

- CASCADE: This will delete all underlying tables from the database
- RESTRICT: This will raise an exception if we run it on a non-empty database

Table and view

In this section, we will be looking at some operations that we can perform on a table and view:

1. Create table: We will be using the following command to create a table:

```
CREATE [EXTERNAL] TABLE [IF NOT EXISTS] [mydb.]mytable
    [(col_name1:col_type1)]
    --[PARTITIONED BY (col_name2:col_type2)]
    [ROW FORMAT row_format]
    [STORED AS file_format]
    [LOCATION path]
    [TBLPROPERTIES (key1=val1, key2=val2, ...)]
    [AS select_statement]
```

Here's an example of creating a table with actual values:

```
CREATE TABLE mytable (id String, firstname String,address String,
city String, State String, zip String, ip String, product_id
String) ROW FORMAT DELIMITED FIELDS TERMINATED BY '\t'
LOCATION '/opt/data'
Stored as TEXTFILE;
```

You will see the following screen on execution of the previous command:

```
spark-sql> CREATE TABLE mytable (id String, firstname String,address String, city String, State String, zip String, ip String, product_id String)
         > ROW FORMAT DELIMITED FIELDS TERMINATED BY '\t'
         > LOCATION '/opt/data'
         > Stored as TEXTFILE;
Time taken: 0.338 seconds
spark-sql> select * from mytable limit 2;
id      firstname      lastname        address city    state   zip     ip
0       Zena    Ross    41228 West India Ln.    Powell  Tennessee       21550   192.168.56.127
Time taken: 2.969 seconds, Fetched 2 row(s)
spark-sql>
```

Here are the parameters that need to be defined during table creation:

- **Datasource**: This is the file format with which this table is associated. It could be CSV, JSON, TEXT, ORC, or Parquet.
- **n**: Specifies the number of buckets if you want to create bucketed table.

2. Create view: We will be using the following command to create a VIEW:

```
CREATE [OR REPLACE] VIEW mydb.myview
    [(col1_name, col2_name)]
    [TBLPROPERTIES (key1=val1, ...)]
    AS select ...
```

This will create a logical view on one or more tables. The view definition will only store the corresponding query definition and, when the view is used, the underlying query will be called at runtime.

3. Describe table: We will be using the following command to DESCRIBE a table:

```
DESCRIBE mydb.mytable
```

Extended: Describe Extended will give more detailed information about the table definition.

4. Alter table or view: There are various operations under ALTER that we can perform. We will be taking a look at the following operations:

- RENAME: We will be using the following command to rename a table or view:

```
ALTER TABLE|VIEW mydb.mytable RENAME TO mydb.mytable1
```

- SET PROPERTIES: The following command can be used to set the properties of a table or view:

```
ALTER TABLE|VIEW mytable SET TBLPROPERTIES (key1=val1,
key2=val2, ...)
```

- Drop properties: The following command can be used to drop the properties of a table or view:

```
ALTER TABLE|VIEW mytable UNSET TBLPROPERTIES IF EXISTS
(key1, key2, ...)
```

5. DROP TABLE: We will be using the following command to drop a table:

```
DROP TABLE mydb.mytable
```

6. This show table properties: We will be using the following command to show the properties of a particular table:

```
SHOW TBLPROPERTIES mydb.mytable [(prop_key)]
```

7. SHOW TABLES: The command that follows is used to show tables:

```
SHOW TABLES [LIKE 'pattern']
```

Shows all tables in the current database. Use pattern if you want to list only specific tables based on a pattern.

8. TRUNACTE TABLE: We will be using the following command to truncate a particular table:

```
TRUNCATE TABLE mytable
```

This will delete all rows from the specified table. It does not work on view or temporary tables.

9. SHOW CREATE TABLE: The following command provides the create table statement for mytable:

   SHOW CREATE TABLE mydb.mytable

10. SHOW COLUMNS: We will be using the following command to display the list of columns in the specified table:

    SHOW COLUMNS (FROM | IN) mydb.mytable

11. INSERT: We will be using the following command to insert values into a table:

    INSERT INTO mydb.mytable select ... from mydb.mytable1

In the event that the table is divided, we must determine a particular partition of the table. We can use the following command to INSERT into PARTITION of a table:

INSERT INTO mydb.mytable PARTITION (part_col_name1=val1) select ... from mydb.mytable1

Load data

We are allowed to load data into Hive tables in three different ways. Two of the methods are DML tasks of Hive. The third is utilizing HDFS order. These three methods are explained as follows:

- **Load data from local filesystem**: We will be using the following command to load data from a local filesystem:

  LOAD DATA LOCAL INPATH 'local_path' INTO TABLE mydb.mytable

  The following screenshot shows how we can load sample_10000.txt from the local filesystem into a Spark table:

```
[spark-sql> LOAD DATA LOCAL INPATH '/opt/data/sample_10000.txt' INTO TABLE mytable;
Time taken: 0.491 seconds
```

- **Load data from HDFS**: We will be using the following command to load data from HDFS:

```
LOAD DATA INPATH 'hdfs_path' INTO TABLE mydb.mytable
```

- **Load data into a partition of a table**: We can use the following command to load data into a partition of a table:

```
LOAD DATA [LOCAL] INPATH 'path' INTO TABLE mydb.mytable PARTITION
(part_col1_name=val1)
```

Creating UDFs

Users can define **User-Defined Functions** (**UDFs**) for custom logic in Scala or Python. The formats for UDF definition and registration are explained as follows:

- The syntax for registering a Spark SQL function as a UDF in Scala is given as follows:

```
val squared = (s: Int) => { s * s }
spark.udf.register("square", squared)
```

- The syntax for calling a Spark SQL function as a UDF in Scala is given as follows:

```
spark.range(1, 20).createOrReplaceTempView(("udf_test"))

%sql select id, square(id) as id_squared from udf_test
```

- The syntax for registering a Spark SQL function as a UDF in Python is given as follows:

```
def squared(s):
  return s * s
spark.udf.register("squaredWithPython", squared)
```

- The syntax for calling a Spark SQL function as a UDF in Python is given as follows:

```
spark.range(1, 20).registerTempTable("test")
%sql select id, squaredWithPython(id) as id_squared from test
```

SQL database using JDBC

Spark SQL also enables users to query directly from different RDBMS data sources. The results of the query are returned as a DataFrame that can be further queried with Spark SQL or joined with other datasets.

To use a JDBC connection, you need to add the JDBC driver jars for the required database in the Spark classpath.

For example, `mysql` can be connected with Spark SQL with the following commands:

```
import org.apache.spark.sql.SparkSession

object JDBCMySQL {
 def main(args: Array[String]) {
 //At first create a Spark Session as the entry point of your app
 val spark:SparkSession = SparkSession
 .builder()
 .appName("JDBC-MYSQL")
 .master("local[*]")
 .config("spark.sql.warehouse.dir", "C:/Spark")
 .getOrCreate();

 val dataframe_mysql = spark.read.format("jdbc")
 .option("url", "jdbc:mysql://localhost:3306/mydb") // mydb is database
name
 .option("driver", "com.mysql.jdbc.Driver")
 .option("dbtable", "mytable") //replace table name
 .option("user", "root") //replace user name
 .option("password", "spark") // replace password
 .load()

 dataframe_mysql.show()
 }
}
```

Summary

In this chapter, we learned how we can connect Spark to the Hive metastore and use the Spark SQL language to perform DDL operations in Spark. Also, we went through how we can connect Spark SQL to different RDBMS datastores and query tables, which provide DataFrames as results. In the next chapter, we will be studying Spark Streaming, machine learning, and graph analysis.

7

Spark Streaming, Machine Learning, and Graph Analysis

In the previous chapter, we learned about Spark SQL, which is one of the core components that provides a SQL interface to query large structured and semi-structured datasets. Spark SQL mainly provide APIs for batch analytics for structured data, but there are domains that need to analyze data streaming data in real time or need to execute a machine learning algorithm on a large volume of train data. Spark provides a different set of APIs based on such application requirements.

This chapter will cover the following topics:

- Spark Streaming
- Machine learning
- Graph APIs

Spark Streaming

Spark Streaming is an extension of core APIs that provide fault-tolerant and high throughput processing of real-time data. It provides APIs that allow the scalable processing of data streams generating at a particular source. The source of the data could be any of the following:

- Click-stream data of websites
- Application logs
- Data coming over a TCP port

Use cases

There are many scenarios where Spark Streaming provides value to an organization, either by enhancing customer experience or proactively monitoring data for recommendations. Different domains where Spark Streaming applications are popular are listed here:

- **Fraud detection**: Financial organizations use Spark Streaming to detect fraudulent transactions in real time. This helps organizations to proactively take a decision on a transaction and to avoid damage in a timely manner.
- **Recommendations**: Domains including e-commerce, media, and others, use Spark Streaming to recommend the next set of products to purchase or the next set of stories to read based on current activities on their platform.
- **Risk avoidance**: Service providers use Spark Streaming to expand their scope of due diligence before offering any service or product. This helps to reduce the risk of providing service or products to non-eligible consumers.

Data sources

Spark Streaming enables developer/analysts to analyze data from a variety of data sources. It provides APIs to connect directly from various messaging queues and TCP ports, including the following:

- **Kafka**
- **Flume**
- **Kinesis**
- **ZeroMQ**
- **Twitter**

Stream processing

The stream of data coming from different data sources is processed in micro-batches. These micro-batches are generated either from data coming directly from a source or from other **DStreams**.

Microbatch

Instead of processing each record or event at a time, Spark receiver's receive data in parallel and keep it in a buffer of Spark worker nodes. Then, Spark's engine runs tasks over these discretized streams, also called microbatches.

A microbatch is created based on a time window, instead of a number of messages.

DStreams

DStreams are the stream of data coming in from a source. A DStream is a continuous series of RDDs where each RDD in DStream contains data from a particular interval. Operations on DStream are translated to operations on underlying RDDs:

Every DStream is associated with a receiver object that receives stream data from a source and stores it in memory for processing.

Streaming architecture

Streaming architecture characterizes how vast of advance through an association. The obtained information is sent to a lot of backend administrations that total the information, sorting out it and making it accessible to business experts, application engineers, and machine learning calculations. The following diagram will help you to understanding the architecture:

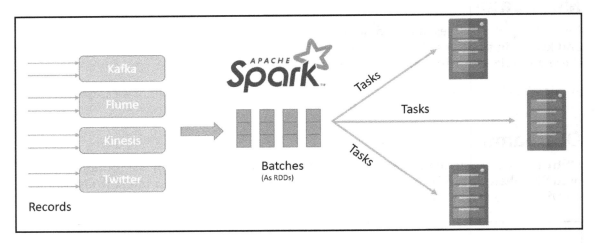

Streaming example

Let's start with a simple word-count example using streaming APIs. As a data source, let's install the NC package on Linux:

```
Installation on CentOS/Red Hat
# Removes the old package
yum erase nc
yum install nc

Installation on Ubuntu
sudo apt-get install netcat
```

The nc or ncat is similar to the cat command but is used for network-streaming data. It is used for reading and writing data across a network.

Start nc on port 8888, as follows:

```
nc -lk 8888
```

The following is the Python code of Spark's Streaming API, to count the stream of words coming over the TCP port:

```python
from pyspark import SparkContext
from pyspark.streaming import StreamingContext

# Create a StreamingContext with two thread on local machine and batch
interval of 1 second

sc = SparkContext("local[2]", "StreamingWC")
ssc = StreamingContext(sc, 1)
lines_stream = ssc.socketTextStream("localhost", 8888)
words = lines_stream.flatMap(lambda line: line.split(" "))
word_pairs = words.map(lambda word: (word, 1))
wordCount = word_pairs.reduceByKey(lambda x, y: x + y)

# Print ten elements of each RDD generated in this DStream to the console
wordCount.pprint()

ssc.start()
ssc.awaitTermination()
```

Create a streaming.py file with the previous code, and run it with the following command:

```
spark-submit --num-executors 1 --executor-memory 1g --total-executor-cores
1 streaming.py
```

You will see the following screen on the execution of the command given:

```
ubuntu@ip-172-31-16-200:/opt$ spark-submit --num-executors 1 --executor-memory 1g --total-executor-cores 1 streaming.py
19/01/19 20:15:59 WARN NativeCodeLoader: Unable to load native-hadoop library for your platform... using builtin-java classes
-------------------------------------------
Time: 2019-01-19 20:16:04
-------------------------------------------


-------------------------------------------
Time: 2019-01-19 20:16:05
-------------------------------------------


-------------------------------------------
Time: 2019-01-19 20:16:06
-------------------------------------------


-------------------------------------------
```

This code listens to any data coming on localhost at port 8888:

```
nc -lk 8888
// on nc terminal send data on 8888
```

You will see the following output on the execution of command given:

```
ubuntu@ip-172-31-16-208:~$ nc -lk 8888
this is spark streaming application. this count streaming words
```

Start sending data over the nc terminal and check for results at Spark Streaming application. You should see the result that follows:

```
---------------------------------------------
Time: 2019-01-19 20:16:22
---------------------------------------------


---------------------------------------------
Time: 2019-01-19 20:16:23
---------------------------------------------
('this', 2)
('is', 1)
('streaming', 2)
('count', 1)
('spark', 1)
('application.', 1)
('words', 1)
```

Machine learning

Machine learning is one of the advanced analytics that harness data. Machine learning is a collection of algorithms that helps people to understand data in many different ways. These algorithms can be categorized into two categories:

- **Supervised learning**: Supervised-learning algorithms are some of the most commonly used machine learning algorithms. They use historical data to train a machine- learning model. These algorithms can be further categorized into classification and regression algorithms. In classification algorithms, the model is trained to predict a categorical/discrete dependent variable. One of the basic examples is predicting whether an email is spam. On the other hand, regression algorithms predict continuous variables. An example of the regression algorithm would be to predict stock prices.

- **Unsupervised learning**: In unsupervised learning, no historical data is used to train a model, rather it tries to find out the hidden patterns in a given data set. One of the famous examples of unsupervised learning is clustering. In clustering algorithms, such as k-means, a model is trained iteratively to find out the different clusters within the data.

Typically, a machine learning use case follows different phases such as data gathering, data cleaning, feature engineering, model training, and testing. The final product of the machine learning process is a model that can be used to predict a dependent variable or to discover data patterns.

As discussed in `Chapter 1`, *Introduction to Apache Spark*, Spark provides **MLlib** and **ML** to work with machine learning. These libraries provide the following:

- A set of common machine learning algorithms, including regression, classification, clustering, and collaborative filtering.
- Features such as extraction, dimensionality reduction, transformation, and pipelines.

MLlib

MLlib is one of the machine learning libraries of Spark. MLlib provides a set of data types that uses RDD to represent data points. Some of the common datatypes are **vectors** and **labeled points**. In MLlib, the supervised algorithm uses RDDs of labeled points and unsupervised algorithm uses vectors to train a model. The MLlib API provides a wide range of machine learning algorithms. Unfortunately, discussing all of them is outside the scope of this book. But, we'll implement one of the supervised learning algorithms and walk you through some of the basic concepts.

One of the most famous supervised learning algorithms is **linear regression**. Before we create our model, let's look at the input data. To understand the algorithm, I have created a small dataset:

```
$ cat train.data
1,10
2,20
3,30
4,40
5,50
```

The previous example shows the content of `train.data` file. It has five rows and two columns. The first column represents a feature vector (independent variable), and the second column is the labeled point (dependent variable). If you look closely, the dependent variable has a linear relationship with the independent variable. We should expect our model to predict a value with the same trend. To test the accuracy of our model, we also have a `test.data` file:

```
$ cat test.data
6,60
7,70
8,80
9,90
```

The following example shows how we can create a linear regression model:

```python
#Python
from pyspark.mllib.regression import LabeledPoint, LinearRegressionWithSGD

#Load and parse the data
def getPoints(line):
    values = [float(x) for x in line.split(',')]
    return LabeledPoint(values[1], [values[0]])


#Read raw data
trainDataRDD = spark.sparkContext.textFile("/FileStore/tables/train.data")
parsedDataRDD = trainDataRDD.map(getPoints)

#Train model
model = LinearRegressionWithSGD.train(parsedDataRDD, iterations=100)


#Test Model
testDataRDD = spark.sparkContext.textFile("/FileStore/tables/test.data")
testParsedDataRDD = testDataRDD.map(getPoints)

actualAndPredRDD = testParsedDataRDD.map(lambda p: (p.label,
model.predict(p.features)))

actualAndPredRDD.collect()
```

Let's go through the previous code in detail. As the first step, we import the `LabeledPoint` and `LinearRegressionWithSGD` classes from the `pyspark.mllib.regression` package. Then, we have defined a function to parse the content of our input files. This function returns a `LabeledPoint` object with it labeled point and feature vector. In our `test.data`, the first value is our feature set and the second value is the labeled point. Next, we use these labeled points to create our `parsedDataRDD`. At this point, our dataset is ready, and we can build our first machine learning model. Next, we use the `train()` method from `LinearRegressionWithSGD` (Stochastic Gradient Descent) library with `parsedDataRDD` and iterations to create our model.

Our model is ready now, and we can test it with our `test.data` file. We first create a `testParsedDataRDD` with similar steps and map it with `predict()` method of our model. Finally, we collect the test results using `collect()`. The following example shows the output of the previous code:

```
Out[49]:    [(60.0, 59.996542573136239),
             (70.0, 69.995966335325619),
             (80.0, 79.995390097514985),
             (90.0, 89.994813859704351)]
```

The output looks as expected. The first value in each tuple is the input feature and the second value is predicted by our model. Our example uses a very small data set. In real-use cases, the data is quite complex, and checking each point is not at all possible. One of the methods to test the accuracy of a machine learning model is the **Mean Squared Error (MSE)** method. The following example shows how to calculate the MSE of a given model:

```python
#Python
#Calculating the mean square error
MSE = actualAndPredRDD \
    .map(lambda vp: (vp[0] - vp[1])**2) \
    .reduce(lambda x, y: x + y) / actualAndPredRDD.count()

print("Mean Squared Error => " + str(MSE))
```

```
Out:Mean Squared Error => 1.90928758278e-05
```

Once a model is finely tuned with the help of different parameters, it can be saved to disk. The following example shows how you can save and load a model in Spark:

```python
#Python

from pyspark.mllib.regression import LinearRegressionModel

#Save
```

```
model.save(spark.sparkContext, "/FileStore/tables/myLRModel")

#load
myModel =
LinearRegressionModel.load(spark.sparkContext,"/FileStore/tables/myLRModel"
)
```

In the previous example, we first imported the `LinearRegressionModel` from the `pyspark.mllib.regression` package. We provided the `sparkContext` and the model location to the `save()` method, which saves our model to disk. You can use `LinearRegressionModel.load()` method to load an existing model into Spark.

ML

As discussed in the previous section, MLlib uses RDD to work with machine learning algorithms, and, therefore, it brings all the disadvantages of RDD. Spark's ML is another library that makes use of the DataFrame API. All the new features have now been added to the ML library, and MLlib is now kept in maintenance mode. Apart from using structured APIs, Spark's ML lets you define the machine- learning *pipeline*, which is similar to the pipeline concept in `scikit-learn`.

Spark ML library provides user-friendly APIs that allow users to combine a set of algorithms into a single pipeline of stages. Each of these stages can perform a separate task (data cleaning, model training, or predicting) and provides an input to the next stage. The pipeline API makes it easy to use a variety of data algorithms in addition to the standard machine learning algorithms. It also supports the ability to save the entire pipeline for later use.

The pipeline API provides two main core features:

- **Transformer**: A transformer takes a DataFrame as input and produces a new DataFrame as an output
- **Estimator**: An estimator is an algorithm that uses a DataFrame to produce a new transformer

A pipeline is just a sequence of these transformers and estimators. The ML library also provides a parameter API that is used by transformers and estimators to specify parameters.

Let's create a decision tree model using ML library:

```scala
//Scala
import org.apache.spark.ml.Pipeline
import org.apache.spark.ml.feature.VectorIndexer
import org.apache.spark.ml.regression.DecisionTreeRegressor

//Load the data using LIBSVM format.
val dataDf =
spark.read.format("libsvm").load("/FileStore/tables/ML/dt.data")

//Split the data into training and test sets (Training Data - 70% | Testing
Data - 30%).
val Array(trainingDataDf, testDataDf) = dataDf.randomSplit(Array(0.7, 0.3))

// Create a feature Indexer [Estimator]
val featureIndexer = new
VectorIndexer().setInputCol("features").setOutputCol("indexedFeatures").fit
(dataDf)

// Train a DecisionTree model [Estimator]
val dtModel = new
DecisionTreeRegressor().setLabelCol("label").setFeaturesCol("indexedFeature
s")

// Create a new pipeline and chain indexer and DecisionTree model into it.
val pipeline = new Pipeline().setStages(Array(featureIndexer, dtModel))

// Train model.
val model = pipeline.fit(trainingDataDf)

// Make predictions.
val predictionsDf = model.transform(testDataDf)

predictionsDf.select("prediction", "label", "features").show(10)
```

In the previous example, we first imported a pipeline and other libraries from
the org.apache.spark.ml package. We then created a DataFrame that holds our input
data. Next, we divided our dataset into training and testing datasets, where 70% of the data
is kept for training our model. We then used an estimator VectorIndexer(),
which automatically identifies categorical features, and indexes them. As the next step, we
defined our decision tree model and used both featureIndexer and dtModel to define a
new pipeline. Finally, a fit() method on the pipeline was called to train our decision tree
model. This step runs both indexer and decision tree estimator.

Once our model is ready, we can use our test data to make some predictions about the labels. For this purpose, we pass `testDataDf` as the parameter to `transform()` method. In the end, we can view both the actual and predicted values by selecting the `prediction` and `label` columns from `predictionsDf`.

`Databricks` has recently launched MLFlow, which can be used to quickly experiment with machine learning models. You can find more details about MLFlow at `https://databricks.com/mlflow`.

Graph processing

In `Chapter 1`, *Introduction to Apache Spark*, we provided a brief introduction to the graph libraries provided by Spark. In this section, we will discuss these libraries in more detail. A graph is one of the data structures that is used in computer science to solve some real-world problems. A graph is represented by a set of *vertices* and *edges*. A vertex is an object, and an edge defines a relationship between two vertices. One of the examples of graphs is a social network, where each person is represented by a vertex, and a relationship between two people is represented by an edge. The following figure shows a graph with five vertices and five edges:

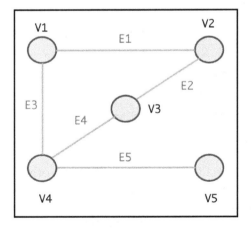

A graph with five vertices and five edges

The graph represented here can also be represented as a set, *V = {V1, V2, V3, V4, V5}* and *E = {E1, E2, E3, E4, E5}*. A graph can also be categorized as a **directed** or **undirected** graph. In the case of a directed graph, the edges also represent a direction from one vertex to another.

Spark's graph library models graphs using an idea called a **property graph**. In a property graph, each vertex is assigned some properties that provide more information about the object represented by the vertex and an edge is also assigned some properties such as weights and relationships. In a property graph, two vertices may share more than one edge. For example, consider the case of the airline industry: each airport can be thought of as a vertex and flights connecting those airports can be represented as edges between them. Two airports might have multiple flights flying in each direction.

Similar to machine learning, graph processing has always been a challenge in the big-data space, as graph algorithms involve lots of data shuffling in distributed mode. Spark addresses these challenges in a unique way and provides two APIs to work with graphs:

- GraphX
- GraphFrames

GraphX

Spark provides the low-level API, **GraphX**, to work with graphs and it makes use of RDDs underneath. Although you may wish to write your own package for graph processing, GraphX comes with some of the optimizations handy. One of the key challenges in graph analysis is data movement. GraphX tackles these challenges by providing features such as the following:

- **Routing table**: This table holds information about partitions that have a reference to a particular vertex
- **Caching of vertex information**: Caching vertex properties for all edge partition data

In GraphX, you store vertex and edge information in RDDs. It is very easy to define a graph in GraphX. All you need is two RDDs representing both vertices and edges. The following example shows how to create a graph using the Scala API:

```scala
//Scala
//Import GraphX
import org.apache.spark.graphx._

//Define a new type VertexId
type VertexId = Long

//Create RDD of vertices
val vertices: RDD[(VertexId, String)] =
spark.sparkContext.parallelize(List((1L, "Sam"),(2L, "John"),(3L,
"Sameer"),(4L, "Alice"),(5L, "Chris")))
```

```
//Create RDD of edges
val edges: RDD[Edge[String]] = spark.sparkContext.parallelize(List(Edge(1L,
2L, "friend"), Edge(1L, 3L, "brother"), Edge(3L, 5L, "brother"), Edge(1L,
4L, "friend"), Edge(4L, 5L, "wife")))

//Finally define a graph
val graph = Graph(vertices, edges)
```

In the previous example, first we import all the modules from
the `org.apache.spark.graphx` package. In addition, we have define a new
type, `VertexId`, which is just an alias to a `Long` type. Next, we define RDDs, which store
all the information about the vertices and edges. Finally, we create a graph by passing both
`vertices` and `edges` as arguments to the `Graph` class.

GraphX also exposes a triplet view, apart from the vertices and edges of a given graph. The
triplet view combines information from both vertices and edge RDDs, and represents a
logical view.

Spark offers a range of operations on a graph. Some of the basic graph operations are
explained in the following sections.

mapVertices

The `mapVertices()` method can be used to map the properties of each vertex of a given
graph. The following example shows the usage of `mapVertices()`:

```
//Scala
//Prefixing 'Hi' with each name
val newGraph = graph.mapVertices((VertexId, name) =>   "Hi "+name )
```

The `mapVertices()` operation is similar to the `mapValues()` transformation. In the
previous example, we just added `'Hi'` to each name of the vertex.

mapEdges

Similar to `mapVertices()`, you can also transform the properties of each edge by using
the `mapEdges()` method on a graph. In the following example, we are modifying relation
attribute of each edge but adding the `"relation"`string:

```
//Scala
val newGraph2 = newGraph.mapEdges( e =>   "relation : "+e.attr )
```

subgraph

One of the important operations of a graph is subgraph(). subgraph() allows users to filter out some of the parts of a graph based on a filter predicate. This predicate can be applied to either a vertex or an edge. The following code example shows how to create a new subgraph by filtering out vertices and edges:

```scala
//Scala
//Filtering the edges which have relation other than 'friend'
val edgeFilterGraph = graph.subgraph(epred = (edge) =>
edge.attr.equals("friend"))
edgeFilterGraph.edges.collect()
```

As shown in the previous example, we are passing an edge predicate (epred) to filter out all the relation expect 'friend' relation. One important point to note here is that all the vertices will still be part of the new edgeFilterGraph. The edge predicate only removes the edges from the edge RDD based on the predicate.

We can also use a vertex predicate to filter out the vertices. In the following example, we are filtering out the vertices that have the name as 'Chris'. In this case, the subgraph method will remove all the edges that link the filtered vertices:

```scala
//Scala
//Filtering out the vertices which have name as 'Chris'
val vertexFilterGraph = graph.subgraph(vpred = (id, name) => !
name.equals("Chris"))
vertexFilterGraph.vertices.collect()
```

For more information on operations offered by GraphX, you can refer to the official Spark documentation.

GraphFrames

Another alternative to GraphX is **GraphFrames**. GraphFrames enjoys all the benefits of structured APIs, as it uses DataFrames underneath. GraphFrames is an external package that can be used with both Scala and Python. You will need to load this package when you start your Spark application. You can download this package from https://spark-packages.org/package/graphframes/graphframes. The following example shows how to include this package while starting a pyspark shell:

```
> $SPARK_HOME/bin/pyspark --packages graphframes:graphframes:0.6.0-
spark2.3-s_2.11
```

We shall use the same data that we used in the GraphX section; the only difference will be that we'll use Python API this time. The procedure to create a graph in GraphFrames is similar to the one we followed in GraphX. The following example shows how to create a graph in GraphFrames:

```Python
#Python
#Importing GraphFrame
from graphframes import GraphFrame

#Creating a DataFrame of vertices
vertices = spark.createDataFrame([(1, 'Sam'),(2, 'John'),(3, 'Sameer'),(4,
'Alice'),(5, 'Chris')],schema=['id','name'])

#Creating a dataframe of edges
edges = spark.createDataFrame([(1, 2, 'friend'),(1, 3, 'brother'),(3, 5,
'brother'),(1, 4, 'friend'),(4, 5, 'wife')],schema=['src','dst', 'attr'])

#Creating a graph
graph = GraphFrame(vertices, edges)
```

In the previous example, we first imported the GraphFrame class from graphframes module. We have then created two DataFrames, vertices and edges. Finally, we used these DataFrames to initialize a graph object using GraphFrame class. Most of the operations provided by GraphFrames are similar to what GraphX provides. Some of the basic methods are explained in the following sections.

degrees

The total number of edges connected to a vertex is known as the **degree** of that vertex. We can use the degrees() method to find out the degree of each vertex of the graph:

```Python
#Python
graph.degrees.show()
```

```
Out:
+---+------+
| id|degree|
+---+------+
| 5 | 2    |
| 1 | 3    |
| 3 | 2    |
| 2 | 1    |
| 4 | 2    |
+---+------+
```

As shown in the previous example, the output of the `degrees()` method is a new DataFrame. In our example, there are five edges, which are connected to the vertex with `id` 1.

subgraphs

Unlike GraphX, GraphFrames does not provide any direct method to create subgraphs, but you can create subgraphs just by writing some filter conditions on either vertices or edges. The following example shows how to `filter` out all the edges that have a relation property other than `"friend"`:

```Python
#Python
#filter out edges with relation other than "friend"
friendsGraph = GraphFrame(graph.vertices, graph.edges.filter("attr ==
'friend'"))
```

 In the previous example, we will only get those edges that have a relation of `"friend"`. The `friendsGraph` will preserve all the vertices of the original graph.

Graph algorithms

This section will provide a brief introduction to some of the algorithms provide by GraphFrames. GraphFrames supports multiple graph algorithms including page rank, triplet count, connected components, breadth-first search, and more. Unfortunately, a discussion on all of these algorithm is out of the scope of this book but, we'll be discussing one of the famous graph algorithms, **PageRank**.

PageRank

The `PageRank` algorithm was designed by founders of Google in 1996. The Google search engine used this algorithm to assign ranks to each web page. `PageRank` was used to rank the web pages based on how many pages point to a given page. This means, the higher the number of links, the higher the importance of the web page. Obviously, `PageRank` is not that simple after all, as there are some other factors that are being used in this algorithm. In our example, we can apply `PageRank` to find out the importance of each person in our graph:

```Python
#Python
from pyspark.sql.functions import desc
```

```
ranks = graph.pageRank(resetProbability=0.15, maxIter=10)
ranks.vertices.orderBy(desc("pagerank")).select("id", "pagerank").show(3)
```

```
Out:
+---+------------------+
| id| pagerank         |
+---+------------------+
| 5 | 1.980701390329944|
| 2 |0.7989209379539325|
| 4 |0.7989209379539325|
+---+------------------+
```

The previous example shows how to find out the top three most important people in our graph. We used the `PageRank` algorithm to first assign the rank to each vertex and then sorted out the vertices based on this rank in descending order.

Summary

In this chapter, we went through the Spark Streaming architecture and created a simple Spark Streaming application. This chapter also covered various MLlib packages that provide APIs to run machine learning applications over Spark.

Lastly, we covered the GraphX APIs, covering GraphFrames and graph algorithms implemented over Spark. In the next chapter, we will look at some optimization techniques to run our Spark code efficiently.

8
Spark Optimizations

In the previous chapters, we learned how to use Spark to implement a variety of use cases using features such as RDDs, DataFrames, Spark SQL, MLlib, GraphX/Graphframes, and Spark Streaming. We also discussed how to monitor your applications to better understand their behavior in production. However, sometimes, you would want your jobs to run efficiently. We measure the efficiency of any job on two parameters: runtime and storage space. In the Spark application, you might also be interested in the statistic of the data shuffles between the nodes. We discussed some of the optimizations in the earlier chapters, but, in this chapter, we'll discuss more optimizations that can help you achieve some performance benefits.

Most developers focus only on writing their applications on Spark and do not focus on optimizing their job for a variety of reasons. This chapter will help developers to choose optimization techniques based on the nature of the bottleneck.

We can categorize the optimizations into two categories:

- Cluster-level optimizations, such as physical hardware and Spark clusters
- Application optimizations

Cluster-level optimizations

As discussed in Chapter 1, *Introduction to Apache Spark*, Spark can scale horizontally. This means that performance will increase if you add more nodes to your cluster, because Spark can perform more operations in parallel. Spark also enables users to take good advantage of memory, and a fast network can also help in optimizing shuffle data. Because of all of these reasons, more hardware is always better.

Memory

Efficient use of memory is critical for good performance. In the earlier versions of Spark, the memory was used for three main purposes:

- RDD storage
- Shuffle and aggregation storage
- User code

Memory was divided among them with some fixed proportions. For example, RDD storage had 60%, shuffle had 20%, and the user code had 20% by default. These properties could be changed by users, depending on the nature of the Spark applications. In the current version of Spark (1.6+), memory management is done automatically.

In the case of caching, we need to be careful when choosing the storage level. The default caching level is MEMORY_ONLY, which keeps the data in memory. If the RDD is big enough and can't fit in memory, then Spark fits as many partitions as it can and, the remaining partitions will be recomputed. This can be avoided if your RDD is expensive to recompute. In such cases, you can use MEMORY_AND_DISK as the storage level. This will move the remaining partitions on the disk and return it to the memory when they are needed without recomputing them.

Disk

A disk is one of the hardware resources used by almost all the applications. Though Spark applications benefit largely from memory, the disk also plays an important role. Spark uses disk space to store the shuffle data temporarily. In Spark standalone mode and Mesos, this location can be configured in SPARK_LOCAL_DIRS variable. In YARN mode, Spark inherits YARN's local directories.

As discussed in Chapter 3, *Spark RDD*, Spark also uses the disk in operations such as checkpointing and caching.

CPU cores

The **central processing unit (CPU)** is the resource where the computation happens. Modern machines come with more than one CPU core, allowing users to run multiple applications in parallel. As discussed in Chapter 5, *Spark Architecture and Application Execution Flow*, tasks for your Spark jobs get executed on these cores. Thus, the degree of parallelism also depends on the number of cores available. This means if you have 1,000 cores available and the total number of partitions is 2,000, then Spark will first schedule the 1,000 tasks for each partition and then run the remaining ones after the completion of the first 1,000 tasks.

We have already discussed how we can control these resources while submitting our job. But it is a good idea to discuss them again in more details. We'll explain this by using an example of a sample cluster. The following diagram shows a cluster of five nodes, each having **16 CPU cores** and **64 GB** of RAM:

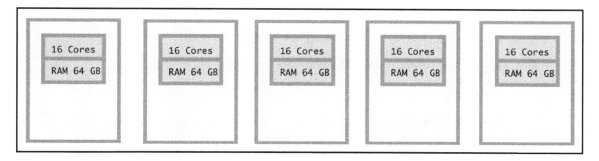

cluster with five nodes

As discussed in Chapter 5, *Spark Architecture and Application Execution Flow,* we can provide resource configurations when the following parameters when submitting our Spark jobs:

- --num-executors: Number of executors
- --executor-cores: Cores assigned to each executor
- --executor-memory: Memory for each executor

While making the decision on the previous configuration, we must take a few things into accounts, such as HDFS I/O throughput and cluster manager resources. One of the ways to choose the right configuration is by trying different combinations and choosing one combination that works best for you, but we'll discuss a way that can help you find a starting point. While reading the data from HDFS, we need to take I/O into account. It seems having a large number of cores for example, 15, can lead to bad I/O throughput. This is because these cores will try to read the same small part of the data on that single machine. Instead, we can have fewer cores (4-6) for each executor to get better throughput. Keeping this in mind, we can calculate the number of executors and memory with the following steps:

1. Calculate the total number of cores available for your Spark application:

   Total number of cores in the cluster = *5 * 16 = 80* cores

   Cores reserved for YARN and others = *1 * 5 =* cores

   Remaining cores available for Spark application = *80 - 5 = 75* core

2. Calculate the total number of executors for your Spark application:

   The possible number of executors = *75 / 5 = 15* executors

   Reserve 1 core for Spark application master(cluster mode) = *15 - 1 = **14***

   executors

3. Calculate the memory for each executor:

   Number of executors running on each node ~ *3* executors

   Memory for each executor = *64 / 3 ~ 21* GB

   Exclude some memory for YARN and heap overhead = *21 - 2 = **19*** GB

This gives us a total of **14** executors for our application, each having 5 CPU cores with **19** GB of memory.

Now it's time to discuss some properties for Spark driver. As Spark driver has the responsibility of DAG construction and task scheduling, sometimes, the driver becomes the bottleneck. You can configure Spark driver to enable dynamic executor allocation. This means Spark can dynamically add or remove executors on the fly. If dynamic executor allocation is enabled and your job has performed an operation such as `coalesce()` and does not require some executors, then the driver will free the resources. Compared to traditional resource allocation, where we have to reserve the resources. This feature brings better resource utilization and can be useful in multi-tenant environments. You can enable it by adding the following properties to your application code:

```
spark.dynamicAllocation.enabled = true
spark.dynamicAllocation.executorIdleTimeout = 2m
spark.dynamicAllocation.minExecutors = 1
spark.dynamicAllocation.maxExecutors = 2000
```

You can also configure the memory allocated to the driver program by setting a flag for `--driver-memory`.

Project Tungsten

This section will discuss **Project Tungsten** and optimizations provided by this project. As a developer, you don't have to configure any property related to Tungsten as Spark provides this optimization by default, but it is worth giving an overview of Tungsten at this point in time. Project Tungsten is all about optimizations. In earlier days of distributed computing, the main bottlenecks in performance were disk I/O and network bandwidth. In recent years, hardware has made a significant improvement. For example, disks are now coming with new options such as **solid state drives** (**SSD**) and flash drives, which has increased disk performance. In a recent study, It was observed that most of the distributed applications do not perform badly because of these reasons; instead, it is the CPU and memory that have become the new bottlenecks.

The goal Project Tungsten is to improve the efficiency of CPU and memory for Spark applications. Three of the main optimizations are the following:

- **Memory management**: This allows Spark to manage memory by eliminating the overhead of **Java virtual machine** (**JVM**) objects that reduces memory consumption and **garbage collection** (**GC**) overhead.

- **Binary processing**: One of the aims of Project Tungsten is to process the data in binary format itself, instead of JVM objects, which are heavier in size. This binary format is known as the `UnsafeRow` format.
- **Code generation**: Using this feature, Spark uses optimization of structured APIs to directly generate the bytecode for your code. This can bring lots of advantages when you write large queries.

Project Tungsten is also home of some other optimizations, such as sorting, join, and shuffle. You can enable or disable Tungsten by using `spark.sql.tungsten.enabled` configuration. For more details on Project Tungsten, please refer the Spark documentation.

Application optimizations

As discussed, there are multiple ways to improve the performance of your Spark applications. In the previous section, we covered some optimizations that were related to hardware. In this section, we'll discuss how you can apply some optimizations while writing your Spark applications.

Language choice

One of the first choices the developers have to make is to decide the language API they are going to write their applications in. In `Chapter 1`, *Introduction to Apache Spark*, we gave an overview of all the languages supported by Spark. The choice of language depends on the use case and the dynamics of the team. If you are part of a data science team and comfortable in writing your machine-learning applications in Python or R, then you might consider Python/R for writing your Spark applications. If you write your code using the structured APIs (DataFrame and Dataset), it is not going to impact performance as at the end the Spark code boils down to RDD code, which doesn't require a Python or R interpreter. One of the recommendations is to write your **user defined functions** (UDF) in Scala. If you are planning to use RDD based on the nature of data, then you might consider writing your applications in Scala or Java to avoid serialization issues.

Structured versus unstructured APIs

We have already discussed the pros and cons of both RDDs and structured APIs. Chapter 3, *Spark RDD*, discussed various reasons why you might choose to write your applications using RDD. Writing your applications in high-level APIs are always better as they bring lots of advantages, but, if you want more physical control of your job, then you can always switch to RDDs. A good practice is to start with the DataFrames/Dataset APIs for the heavy computation, and then use RDD to get better control of your application.

File format choice

Your choice of file format can also impact the performance of your Spark applications. You should consider three parameters while choosing the file format for your application:

- Binary versus text
- Splittable versus non-splittable
- Column versus row-based

Binary file formats improve both storages and network transfer. The binary format has a higher rate of compression compared to a text-based file format such as CSV and JSON. You should always choose a splittable file format. This allows different tasks to read a different part of the data in parallel.

The choice between columnar file format and row based file format depends upon the access pattern of the data. If your access pattern suggests frequent read and computes only on specific fields, then column-based file formats are good choices. For example, if you have an employee dataset that has fields such as emp_id, emp_name, salary, and date_of_joining, and you compute only aggregate salary most of the time, then columnar file formats such as Parquet and ORC can be the best choice for your application.

Columnar file formats also have a high rate of compression. Spark recommends storing your data in Parquet or ORC format.

RDD optimizations

In this section, we'll discuss some optimizations on RDDs.

Choosing the right transformations

One of the ways to optimize your applications is to avoid the shuffling of your data. Lesser the shuffle, less in the execution time. If you choose your transformations carefully, then you can avoid heavy data shuffles. For example, let's assume you have an RDD of tuples (pair RDD) having the first element as an alphabet and the second element a numeric value. You want to compute the sum of all the elements of the RDD based on the keys. There are many ways to do that but, let's look at two of the choices:

- groupByKey()

```
//groupByKey()
val rawData = Array(("A",1),("B",1),("C",1),("A",2),("B",1))
val baseRDD = spark.sparkContext.parallelize(rawData)
baseRDD.groupByKey().mapValues(_.sum).collect()

//Output
res20: Array[(String, Int)] = Array((A,3), (B,2), (C,1))
```

In the preceding code, we first created an array `rawData`. This array had some tuples in it. We then parallelized this collection to create our first RDD (`baseRDD`). We then used `groupByKey()` to group data with similar keys together and then ran the `mapValues()` transformation to sum up all the elements for each key. Finally, we collected the result using `collect()`.

- reduceByKey()

The following example code uses `reduceByKey()` instead of `groupByKey()`:

```
//reduceByKey()
baseRDD.reduceByKey( _+_ ).collect()

//Output
res14: Array[(String, Int)] = Array((A,3), (B,2), (C,1))
```

Though both the approaches result in the same output, there is a difference between how each of these transformations processes the data. In the case of `groupByKey()`, the data will be shuffled across nodes based on the key. Once the data is available on each node, we can aggregate the data using a `mapValues()` transformation. On the other hand, if `reduceByKey()` data is first aggregated locally on each node, then it is transferred to other nodes based on the key. This way, `reduceByKey()` shuffles less data compared to `groupByKey()`. In some cases, when your data is highly skewed, you might face issues with `groupByKey()` because all the records with the same key will be sent to a single machine.

In our example, the data used was very small, which is why you might not see the difference between the execution time, but, in the case of larger datasets, it does make a difference. You can also use Spark UI to check the amount of data, which gets shuffled during the execution.

You should always consider using `filter()` transformation before applying any wide transformation.

Serializing and compressing

Whenever we use custom data types in our Spark application, we should serialize them. Java serialization is the default serialization but, changing the serialization format to Kryo can increase the performance. Objects serialized by Java serializer are often slow and larger in size as compared to the Kryo serializer. You can change the `spark.serializer` property to `org.apache.spark.serializer.KryoSerializer` to set the Kryo serializer. You would require your class to register with the Kryo and you can be strict about class registration. In the following example, we first mandate the class registration by setting the flag `spark.kryo.registrationRequired` to `true`. We then register two of our classes in Scala:

```Scala
//Scala
conf.set("spark.kryo.registrationRequired", "true")
conf.registerKryoClasses(Array(ClassOf[FirstCustomClass],ClassOf[SecondCust
omClass]))
```

This serialization information will be used during the shuffle phase as well as when writing the data to disk. You can also choose compression such as snappy or LZF which can compress the data to a great extent and can improve the shuffle performance.

Broadcast variables

Before we explain the broadcast variable, let's discuss the concept of closures. Let's take a simple example:

```Python
#Python
spark.sparkContext.parallelize(range(1,11))\
                  .map(lambda x : x*2)\
                  .collect()

#Output
Out[4]: [2, 4, 6, 8, 10, 12, 14, 16, 18, 20]
```

In the previous example, we first created an RDD by using `parallelize()` method and then we multiplied each element by 2 to generate the even numbers. Under the hood, when Spark driver schedules the tasks, each task has a copy of the function (`lambda x: x*2`) along with the data that function uses (in our example: 2). This means each task will have a copy of the number 2. In our example, you might not notice any performance bottleneck as our data size is very small and also we are just multiplying an integer but, imagine running similar operations on a very large RDD, which used a large variable inside the function. This will increase both the task shipping time and the memory space on the executors, as each task will have its own copy of the variable.

To avoid this scenario, Spark provides `broadcast` variables. The `broadcast` variables are only copied once to each executor and then tasks can use that copy for computation. This improves both run time and storage space. The following example uses `broadcast`. We first `broadcast` number 2 to all the executor using `broadcast()` and give it a reference `numberTwo`. We then use `numberTwo.value` to access the actual value during the `map()` transformation:

```
#Python
numberTwo = spark.sparkContext.broadcast(2)
spark.sparkContext.parallelize(range(1,11))\
                  .map(lambda x : x*numberTwo.value)\
                  .collect()

#Output
Out[5]: [2, 4, 6, 8, 10, 12, 14, 16, 18, 20]
```

The `broadcast` variables are read-only variables. Spark also provides **accumulators** that are equivalent to counters in map reduce. Accumulators are the write-only variables and can be used to get statistics such as the number of bad records in the input file while running your application. Please refer Spark documentation for more details on accumulators.

DataFrame and dataset optimizations

This section will discuss some optimization techniques that you can use while working with the structured APIs.

Catalyst optimizer

One of the components that work with Spark structured API is **Catalyst Optimizer**. The aim of the catalyst optimizer is to provide performance benefits for structured APIs such as SQL, DataFrame, and dataset. The idea is that when you have schema information, you can optimize the query plan. For each query submitted by the user, it first gets converted to a **Logical Query plan**. This **Logical Query plan** has high-level information about the query in form of a tree of expressions and operations. Catalyst optimizer then performs a series of transformations on this logical plan to come up with the most efficient and **Optimized Query plan**. This optimized **Logical Query plan** is then converted to *a physical query plan*. The physical query plan also has similar information as a logical plan but has some extra information such as which file to read or which join to perform. Finally, the project Tungsten will generate the RDD code for the input query. The following diagram shows the previous series of steps:

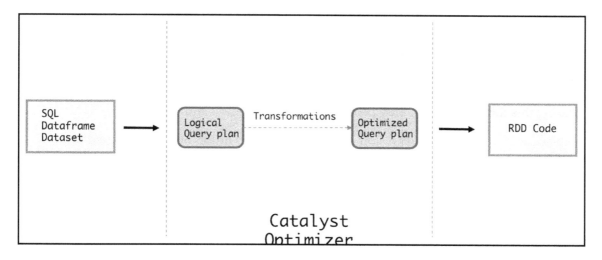

Catalyst Optimizer

In the preceding diagram, once a Spark SQL query, a DataFrame, or a dataset code is submitted, the **Catalyst Optimizer** receives a **Logical Query plan**. **Catalyst Optimizer** and then performs some transformations on it to drive the optimized versions of it. These optimizations might include pushing down a predicate to the data source, evaluating a constant operation (for example 5+6 = 11) only once or choosing a right type of join. The optimized query plan is then submitted to Tungsten to generate the equivalent RDD code.

You can refer databricks blogs for more details on the catalyst optimizer.

Storage

The way you store your data decides how fast you are going to retrieve it. It is always better to choose some partition or bucketing strategies that can help you process your data faster. Spark provides both partition and bucketing while storing the DataFrames. In the case of *partitioning*, the files are created under directories based on a key field. For example, you can choose a data field to partition your data. One thing to keep in mind when working with partitioning is that the key field should have low cardinality; that is, the field should have lesser possible values. If the cardinality were too high, you would end up creating a large number of partitions that can become a bottleneck, as so many tasks are launched to process those partitions. Ideally, a partition should have at least 128 MB of data. At the time reading this data, Spark will only process the given partition and ignore the rest.

In the case of higher cardinality, you can use *bucketing* to group and store related keys together. If two tables are bucketed on the same fields and have an equal (multiple) numbers of buckets then joining these two tables on the same fields will take lesser time when compared to joining them without the buckets.

Parallelism

The default number of shuffle partitions in Spark SQL is 200. It means if you use a transformation that shuffles the data, you would have 200 shuffle blocks as an output. If your data is huge and you still use the default setting of `spark.sql.shuffle.partitions` then the shuffle blocks will have a high block size. In Spark, the size of the shuffle block cannot be greater than 2 GB. This might lead to a run time exception. To avoid such exceptions, you should always consider increasing the number of shuffle partitions. This will eventually decrease the size of the shuffle partitions. The ideal size of a partition is close to 128 MB. In Spark SQL, you can change the size of the shuffle blocks by changing the value of `spark.sql.shuffle.partitions`. In RDD, you should consider `repartition()` or `coalesce()` for changing the number of partitions.

Join performance

Spark SQL provides a variety of joins, such as the following:

- Shuffle hash join
- Broadcast hash join
- Cartesian join

If the size of both the tables is large and they both are bucketed/partitioned on the same joining field, then shuffle hash join can best suit your needs. It works best when the data is evenly distributed based on the key field and there are enough unique values for that key field to achieve the necessary parallelism. If one of the tables is small in size, you can use broadcast join, which caches the small data on each machine and avoids shuffle.

Code generation

As discussed earlier in this chapter, Spark can generate bytecode for your queries on the fly. Spark compiles each query to its Java bytecode equivalent code when `spark.sql.codegen` is set to `true`. By default, this property is set as `false`. In case your queries are big, you can set this property to true to improve on performance.

Speculative execution

If your jobs are running slowly, and from Spark UI you find out that some of the tasks are running slower when compared to others, then you might consider enabling speculation execution for these tasks. If the property `spark.speculation` is set to true, then Spark will identify the slow running tasks and run the speculative tasks on other nodes to complete the job more quickly. The tasks that finish first are accepted and the second task gets killed by Spark.

The following code sets this property to `true`:

```python
#Python
conf.set("spark.speculation","true")
```

Summary

In this chapter, we discussed some of the optimizations provided by Spark. First, we discussed some hardware level optimizations, such as setting the number of cores, executors, and the amount of memory for your Spark applications. We then gave an overview of project Tungsten and its optimizations. Then, we covered application-level optimizations, such as choosing the right language, API and the file format for your applications. Finally, we covered optimizations provided by RDD and DataFrame APIs.

This is the end of this book. I thank you for staying with me till the end, and I hope you enjoyed the content. If you wish to explore Apache Spark in more detail, you may also consider buying *Learning Apache Spark 2*, by Packt.

Other Books You May Enjoy

If you enjoyed this book, you may be interested in these other books by Packt:

Big Data Analytics Using Apache Spark [Video]
Arokia Armel

ISBN: 9781789134124

- Easy data computation via Spark SQL.
- Learn basic Spark functionalities
- Achieve efficient task scheduling, memory management, and fault recovery with Spark components
- Adopt the right framework for better performance.
- Provide uniform wrapping across all data access with SparkSession.
- Attain fast data processing on your unstructured data with Spark RDD.
- Achieve high-level abstraction with DataFrames, Datasets, and structured/semi-structured data.

Machine Learning with Apache Spark Quick Start Guide
Jillur Quddus

ISBN: 9781789346565

- Understand how Spark fits in the context of the big data ecosystem
- Understand how to deploy and configure a local development environment using Apache Spark
- Understand how to design supervised and unsupervised learning models
- Build models to perform NLP, deep learning, and cognitive services using Spark ML libraries
- Design real-time machine learning pipelines in Apache Spark
- Become familiar with advanced techniques for processing a large volume of data by applying machine learning algorithms

Leave a review - let other readers know what you think

Please share your thoughts on this book with others by leaving a review on the site that you bought it from. If you purchased the book from Amazon, please leave us an honest review on this book's Amazon page. This is vital so that other potential readers can see and use your unbiased opinion to make purchasing decisions, we can understand what our customers think about our products, and our authors can see your feedback on the title that they have worked with Packt to create. It will only take a few minutes of your time, but is valuable to other potential customers, our authors, and Packt. Thank you!

Index

narrow transformations 43
wide transformations 46
transformer 112
types, Resilient Distributed Dataset (RDD)
about 53
pair RDD 53

U

undirected graph 114
UnsafeRow format 126
unsupervised learning 109
user defined functions (UDF) 100, 126

V

vectors 109
vertex 114

W

wide transformations
about 46
cartesian() 48, 49
distinct() 47
intersection() 47
sortBy() 47
subtract() 48

Y

Yet Another Resource Negotiator (YARN) 6, 16

www.ingramcontent.com/pod-product-compliance
Lightning Source LLC
Chambersburg PA
CBHW080535060326
40690CB00022B/5133